Language and Human Action

Studies in the Humanities
Literature—Politics—Society

Guy Mermier
General Editor

Vol. 12

PETER LANG
New York • Washington, D.C./Baltimore
Bern • Frankfurt am Main • Berlin • Vienna • Paris

R. A. Watson

Language and Human Action

Conceptions of Language in the *Essais* of Montaigne

PETER LANG
New York • Washington, D.C./Baltimore
Bern • Frankfurt am Main • Berlin • Vienna • Paris

Library of Congress Cataloging-in-Publication Data

Watson, R.A.
Language and human action: conceptions of language in the essais
of Montaigne/ R.A. Watson.
p. cm. — (Studies in the humanities; vol. 12)
English, French and German.
Includes bibliographical references.
1. Montaigne, Michel de, 1533–1592. Essais. 2. Montaigne, Michel de, 1533–1592—Knowledge—Language and languages. 3. French essays—History and criticism. 4. Act (Philosophy) in literature. I. Title. II. Series: Studies in the humanities (New York, N.Y.); vol. 12.
PQ1643.W38 844'.3—dc20 93-467
ISBN 0-8204-1987-7
ISSN 0742-6712

Die Deutsche Bibliothek-CIP-Einheitsaufnahme

Watson, Richard A.:
Language and human action: conceptions of language in the essais of Montaigne/ R.A. Watson. –New York; Washington, D.C./Baltimore; Bern; Frankfurt am Main; Berlin; Vienna; Paris: Lang.
(Studies in the humanities; Vol. 12)
ISBN 0-8204-1987-7
NE: GT

Cover design by James F. Brisson.

TO MY FATHER AND MOTHER
WITH LOVE AND GRATITUDE

ACKNOWLEDGEMENTS

I would like to express my sincere appreciation to:

Professor Barbara C. Bowen for directing the dissertation from which this book is adopted;

The Presses Universitaires de France for their kind permission to quote from *Les Essais*, editor Pierre Villey;

Michael Moore for proofreading.

TABLE OF CONTENTS

INTRODUCTION

This study proposes to examine and elucidate Montaigne's conceptions of language by means of an analysis of apposite passages in the *Essais*. Upon close reading, one becomes aware that Montaigne's views on language, while unarguably coherent, are composed of elements qualitatively unlike. Confronted with a great number of such differences, I have sought a simple yet comprehensive method of ordering them. This requisite form is an attributive distinction among intellectual, moral, and artistic aspects. Such a distinction is not new: its usefulness has been demonstrated by both Traeger in *Aufbau und Gedankenführung in Montaignes Essays*[1] and Bowen in *The Age of Bluff: Paradox and Ambiguity in Rabelais and Montaigne.*[2] Thus, all disparate elements of Montaigne's judgments on language may be grouped under one of these basic headings. Pursuing a further analysis within each category, I have identified several subjects or themes each of which constitutes a single aspect of the three basic general qualities. According to criteria of diminishing scope and complexity, the intellectual field will be treated first, followed by the moral and artistic, respectively. We may further clarify the distinction among these three areas by introducing certain principles of definition hitherto developed in Montaigne criticism. Traeger, for example, has recourse to a virtually identical tri-partite distinction:

> Wir können weiter die schon dargestellten drei Formen unterscheiden, in denen das Ich sich bietet: als Denkender tritt Montaigne beständig auf; die Ichform der Urteile ist ebenso nachdrücklich betont wie in den langen Essais der vorhergehenden Schaffensperiode. Vielfach spricht Montaigne—so im fünften und neunten Essai—von sich als Verfasser des Werks, das der Leser vor sich hat. Als Lebender endlich stellt er sich nicht nur immer wieder vor, sondern eine Reihe von drei Essais ist durch ein biographisches Band verknüpft: Montaigne spricht von seiner großen Reise (1580-81); von seinem Amt als Bürgermeister von Bordeaux (1581-85); von seiner schwierigen Lage zwischen den kämpfenden Parteien der Religionsfehden und seiner Flucht vor der Pest (1586-87). Diese autobiographischen Anlässe werden zum Ausgangspunkt der allgemeinen Fragestellungen und Betrachtungen....[3]

These three forms of Montaigne's thought present in the *Essais* may obviously be extrapolated into the more abstract and less personal triple perspective set forth above. Thus the *Denkender* creates the intellectual; the

Lebender, the moral; and the *Verfasser*, the artistic content. Likewise, the intellectual aspect of language may be designated as ideational, theoretical content; the moral, as practical, contingent, and derivative content; and the artistic, as the form which the language, bearer of the content, ultimately assumes. The correspondence between the terms of Traeger's analysis and those previously adduced is striking: the thinker produces the ideal content; the living man, the practical or routine content; and the author, the literary form.

Bowen evokes these three generalizations in much the same fashion as I propose to do. She distinguishes three planes of understanding intrinsically present in Montaigne's work: i.e., the intellectual, the moral, and the artistic: "Montaigne, like many educated people of his time and ours, has three main concerns, one moral, one intellectual, and one artistic."[4]

The foregoing, of course, may be described in traditional terms of basic critical concepts derived from Aristotle. The three modes of action—doing, making, and contemplation—provide a rough classification of all human actions. *Praxis*, *poiesis*, and *theoria* thus form a classification which parallels and mirrors those set forth above.

It is thus apparent that this framework of enquiry is neither capricious nor arbitrary, nor even external to the work itself, but rather imposes itself resolved into its constituent parts, layers interwoven within the fabric of the *Essais*.

Two critics have recently treated the topic of Montaigne's conception of language at length and in detail. The findings of two others as well—in particular of Friedrich—may serve to establish a frame of reference with which to compare and contrast my own study.

In *Montaigne*[5] Friedrich situates Montaigne in the current of reaction to the early Italian humanists' unquestioning espousal and imitation of classical literary form. For Friedrich, theory and practice happily coincide in Montaigne's composition, yet clearly stand apart from the traditional rhetoric of the schoolmen. He further holds that Montaigne, eschewing strictly defined terms, purposefully uses instead hazy and equivocal ones; and that semantic nuances derive from context rather than from traditional usage. Montaigne's style is the *stilus comicus*, the lowest of the three classical styles. Finally, Friedrich affirms Montaigne's nominalist and skeptical criticism of language.

In an article entitled "Language and the Dialectic of the Self in Montaigne's *Essais*,"[6] Regosin deals with Montaigne's conception of language on both a philosophical and an esthetic level. Since language is only a symbol, it is by the same token only a semblance of the thought it seeks to define. An imperfect epistemological tool, its craft may forge error as well as truth. It is *per se* ambiguous. Words are also ontologically different and distinct from their meaning. Montaigne tries to close these distances by reworking and renewing terminology. Most significantly, Montaigne vitalizes language with concrete and sensual terminology and metaphor.

As set forth in her thesis entitled "Expression and Being and the *Essais* of Montaigne,"[7] Winegrad's interpretation of language in the *Essais* is grounded in two pairs of basic concepts which define and describe the term itself: namely, expression and being on the one hand, and theme and image on the other.[8] Language is *the* immediate expression of Montaigne as well as the means to his end of being. In a like manner, language is *an* immediate theme as well as the means to his end of image. Thus, Montaigne first of all comes to life in his work, and secondly this existence is wrought in the self-portrait or the literary image of the author. Language thereby touches upon every aspect of the *Essais*: "Language is a natural addendum to any other consideration because of the particular nature of the *Essais*."[9] Winegrad further elaborates the foregoing principles of her argument in a series of abstractions which are complementary or contradictory with respect to one another, such as form and substance, externals and essentials, language and concepts, *le nom et la chose*, philosophy and philology, etc. This dialectical development allows a deeper penetration and more detailed analysis of the subject. The final synthesis or resolution[10] Winegrad terms integrity. She envisions Montaigne's concept of language and his language itself as the reconciliation or harmonious orchestration of various antinomies which are its logical components. They are brought together in such a way as to point up the predominantly moral quality of the self-portrait, its truthfulness and faithfulness.

Ehrlich's study, *Montaigne: la critique et le langage*,[11] while resembling those discussed above with respect to certain universally received findings of Montanist criticism, differs from them with regard to critical method as well as emphasis. She approaches the *Essais* from a modernist perspective and thereby discovers hitherto unsuspected affinities between Montaigne's conception and use of language and certain linguistic and psychological theories which have gained wide currency in some quarters today. She ascribes a single governing intention or motivation to Montaigne's language, namely, that of criticizing and correcting corruption and hypocrisy by revealing the ambiguity inherent in language with which these ills cloak themselves. For ambiguity is the quality which permits words to be misappropriated, thereby creating and propagating falsehoods to the detriment of the social, political, and religious orders. Furthermore, she stresses the role of the mask and game metaphors in conveying and seconding Montaigne's moral preoccupation with language as well as the exemplary function of the self-portrait (calculated as a counterweight to false or insincere revelation or declaration). Ehrlich agrees with Friedrich in the matter of Montaigne's theoretical and pragmatic aversion to Ciceronian rhetoric; she characterizes his language as poetic and connotative, presumably as opposed to prosaic and denotative.

My study seeks to discover and to clarify Montaigne's conceptions of language by interrogating the *Essais* themselves. These conceptions have of course already been dealt with, notably by the four critics mentioned above, but also in a less comprehensive or specific manner by a host of others as well. Nor does the methodology of my enquiry lay any claim to originality. Its uniqueness lies rather in its treatment of the subject: no one has sought to approach the problem of language through the three personnages of the author named by Traeger and corresponding objectively to the planes or levels employed by Traeger and Bowen. Such a procedure permits a system of classification which, if it casts the same light, does project it from a new angle. Essentially, I wish to restrict the compass of the topic to Montaigne's conception of or attitude toward language rather than his use of it. The questions concerning style and composition have been adequately and thoroughly treated elsewhere. Within the scope of our study, we will, however, be able to offer responses to several important questions which have been raised concerning our topic. The body of this work consists of a question and answer dialogue with the text of the *Essais*. This exchange is articulated and modulated by certain dual philosophical principles, such as cause and effect, truth and error, reason and emotion, thought and expression, man and society, life and death, and nature and metaphysics.

In addition, I do not intend to treat the question of rhetoric, at least in its traditional sense. To include a subject of its magnitude and depth would carry this study beyond acceptable bounds. Also, for practical reasons such as brevity, coherence, consistency of purpose, and avoidance of intricate complexity, I exclude the strata question. Indeed, this problem has already been much discussed and at great length, possibly giving rise to more obfuscation than clarification, particularly with regard to Villey's evolutionary thesis and the adverse stance adopted by many later critics. In accordance with the focus and thrust of my study, I prefer to elaborate the content and form of Montaigne's concepts of language by a close examination of the text, without addressing myself to questions of development or chronology. I feel that to do otherwise would be to take the parts for the whole, to spuriously fragmentize an integral text. Moreover, the necessarily tenuous nature of whatever conclusion might be thereby attained, as evidenced by the contradiction of critical opinion on this point, discourages its pursuit in this initial and modest undertaking.

The first chapter, treating Montaigne's intellectual concepts of language, is subdivided into eight categories, each of which discusses one aspect of the general heading. The sequence of their arrangement is the most logical I have found possible and attempts to retrace as nearly as possible Montaigne's own processes of ideational association as conveyed in the *Essais*.

All references to the *Essais* are taken from *Les Essais*, édition P. Villey (réimprimée sous la direction et avec une préface de V.-L. Saulnier), Paris: Presses Universitaires de France, 1965. Page references are preceded by the book number in Roman capitals followed by the chapter in Arabic numerals.

CHAPTER I

The Language Of Intellectual Action: The Attempt At a Statement Of Truth

Depicting Interior Reality: Style and Structure in the *Essais*

The Adoption of a Style of Self-Revelation

Unlike a photograph which renders a one-dimensional image, sterile and lifeless, showing us a person embalmed with all the juices and vitality drained, Montaigne's style is enlivened by his personality and character. It is neither flat nor unreal, but rather, in his attempt to reveal himself he has succeeded in drawing a portrait of his psychosynthesis which moves and lives throughout his work. The image which emerges is as alive and real as the people we know in our own lives. To read his *Essais* is to have a conversation with him:

> Ich vermute, daß jeder, der sich in Montaigne eingelesen hat, die gleiche Erfahrung macht wie ich: nachdem ich ihn einige Zeit gelesen und einige Vertrautheit mit seiner Art erworben hatte, meinte ich ihn sprechen zu hören und seine Gesten zu sehen.[12]

> Das alles sind Eigentümlichkeiten, die man weit eher in der Unterhaltung (freilich nur mit ganz besonders gedanken- und ausdrucksreichen Menschen) zu finden gewohnt ist als in einer gedruckten Schrift theoretischen Inhalts; man meint, für eine solche Wirkung sei Tonfall, Geste und die gegenseitige Erwärmung, die eine erfreuliche Unterhaltung mit sich bringt, unerläßlich. Aber Montaigne, der mit sich allein ist, findet in seinem Denken genug Leben und gleichsam körperliche Wärme, um zu schreiben, als ob er spräche.[13]

Certainly Traeger's reaction to Montaigne's work mirrors that of many Montaigne critics; indeed, Montaigne himself writes: "J'ose non seulement parler de moy, mais parler seulement de moy: je fourvoye quand j'escry d'autre chose et me desrobe à mon subject. Je ne m'ayme pas si indiscretement et ne suis si attaché et meslé à moy que je ne me puisse distinguer et considerer à quartier: comme un voisin, comme un arbre." (III 8 942 C) Montaigne thereby advances and affirms his choice of himself as the proper subject of the *Essais*. The foregoing statement suggests a vivid style which is never static. In fact, Montaigne's style is as alive and developing as his character; and it evolves and solidifies gradually throughout the course of his writing and his intellectual life. Parslow informs us that it is not until the third book of the *Essais* that "...the ultimate in self-portrayal—composition as representation—is fully realized."[14]

The person who emerges from the *Essais* is garrulous and outgoing, a social creature who needs to fulfill himself by communicating with others of equal intellectual stature and similar character: "Les hommes de la societé et familiarité desquels je suis en queste, sont ceux qu'on appelle honnestes et habiles hommes: l'image de ceux cy me degouste des autres." (III 8 824 B) "Je suis sociable jusques à excez." (III 9 982 C) "Je suis affamé de me faire connoistre; et ne me chaut à combien, pourveu que ce soit veritablement." (III 5 847 B) He goes on to say that he finds it difficult to "...me communiquer à demy et avec modification." (III 3 821 B) "Ma forme essentielle est propre à la communication et à la production: je suis tout au dehors et en evidence, nay à la societé et à l'amitié." (III 3 823 B)

In his early years his friendship with La Boétie serves as an outlet for the discussion of his most intimate ideas and feelings. Frame states: "If La Boétie had lived,, Montaigne would probably have written in the form of letters."[15] Montaigne himself states: "(B) Sur ce subject de lettres, je veux dire ce mot, que c'est un ouvrage auquel mes amys tiennent que je puis quelque chose. Et eusse prins plus volontiers ceste forme à publier mes verves, si j'eusse eu à qui parler." (I 40 252) The *Essais* may have been in a sense a result of La Boétie's death: they are a kind of conversation with the self. After La Boétie's death Montaigne's solitude and his feeling of isolation inspire him to write, but first he has to introduce an essayistic form suitable to his reflections. He seeks a unique way to express himself "...that would be both a testimony to his life and a means of communication which might bring him another good friend...."[16]

In this manner, Montaigne's style of writing begins to evolve. In essence, the *Essais* become a journey into the self based on his desire to understand his own motivations more completely. He considers the direct result of conversation to be the edification of the self and a quest for self-knowledge. In effect, Montaigne "...sat down to write his essays to give clarity, order, and stability to his own thoughts; he wrote to give himself a firm shape."[17]

From projecting himself into an object for study, Montaigne moves to a realization that self-study is important because of what it can teach us concerning ourselves as human beings living in the world: "Je ne fay nulle recepte des biens que je n'ay peu employer à l'usage de ma vie. Quel que je soye, je le veux estre ailleurs qu'en papier. Mon art et mon industrie ont esté employez à me faire valoir moy-mesme; mes estudes, à m'apprendre à faire, non pas à escrire. J'ay mis tous mes efforts à former ma vie. Voylà mon mestier et mon ouvrage." (II 37 784 A)

Of course, in Montaigne's time the idea of self-study or self-portrayal is a radical one, and Montaigne proceeds with caution in constructing his plan. "It seems to have been only around 1578 that Montaigne first found the title of his work. Although the best account of his plan cannot be dated, all the others are of 1578 or later. The term 'essay' (*essai)* was his own invention, tentative in every way, not yet crystallized or hackneyed."[18] By and large, the term refers to the trying out or testing of ideas through experience. Montaigne is portrayed as one particular man living his life and experiencing the joy and sorrow of being human. Consequently, he assumes his readers will find similarities between his life and their own. He is not depicting man in the abstract, but rather, he is studying a concrete, living individual. His generalizations always stem from his own personal experience.

The *Essais* and the Ancients: A Departure

Most contemporary writers feel great reverence for their ancient predecessors, as evidenced by the appearance of many collections of their works. Montaigne feels this is a poor substitute for personal judgment and experience. He requires a certain freedom from the past's preconceptions in order for his view of the relative nature of truths to operate. This is the basis of his criticism of an undue adherence to the Ancients. He believes we should use our own experience and give credit to the evidence of our own lives: "Ou bien certes, que nous n'avons pas l'esprit d'esplucher et faire valoir ce qui se passe devant nous, et le juger assez vifvement pour le tirer en exemple?" (III 13 1081 B) In addition, there are far too many interpretations of the Ancients: "Je dis souvent que c'est pure sottise qui nous fait courir apres les exemples estrangers et scholastiques. Leur fertilité est pareille à cette heure à celle du temps d'Homere et de Platon." (III 13 1081 B) Furthermore, he justifies the use of himself as the subject of his writing: "Quel que soit donq le fruict que nous pouvons avoir de l'experience, à peine servira beaucoup à nostre institution celle que nous tirons des exemples extrangers, si nous faisons si mal nostre proffict de celle que nous avons de nous mesme, qui nous est plus familiere, et certes suffisante à nous instruire de ce qu'il nous faut. Je m'estudie plus qu'autre subject. C'est ma metaphisique, c'est ma phisique." (III 13 1072 B)

Although he too uses quotations of and references to the Ancients, Montaigne absorbs what he reads and changes it according to his own outlook and experiences: "Je feuillette les livres, je ne les estudie pas: ce qui m'en demeure, c'est chose que je ne reconnois plus estre d'autruy; c'est cela seulement dequoy il s'est imbu; l'autheur, le lieu, les mots et autres circonstances, je les oublie incontinent." (II 17 651 A) He considers the words and thoughts of the Ancients as well as those of his contemporaries, but these are only some of the things which pass through his mind and return to us stamped with his unique imprint. He appears to absorb all that takes place about him, what he reads and what he sees and hears. He continually employs all the material he assembles for his writing in a personal and innovative way. In fact, he ridicules unoriginal writers who only ape the Ancients: "Nous sçavons dire: Cicero dit ainsi; voilà les meurs de Platon: ce sont les mots mesmes d'Aristote. Mais nous, que disons nous nous mesmes? que jugeons nous? que faisons nous? Autant en diroit bien un perroquet." (I 25 137 A)

The Rhetoric of Self-Revelation

Although his subject is of primary importance to him, the language which he employs in his work is another consideration for him and one which is directly connected to the concept of self-study. He says: "Car, quelque langue que parlent mes livres, je leur parle en la mienne." (II 10 418 A) An examination of Montaigne's writings appears to reveal the truth of this statement. And, after all, "Montaigne is the best authority we have on the subject of his own way of writing."[19] He states further: "(A) Je n'ayme point de tissure où les liaisons et les coutures paroissent, tout ainsi qu'en un beau corps, il ne faut qu'on y puisse compter les os et les veines. '*Quae veritati operam dat oratio, incomposita sit et simplex.*' '*Quis accurate loquitur, nisi qui vult putide loqui*?' L'éloquence faict injure aux choses, qui nous destourne à soy." (I 26 172) Furthermore, "Or, autant que la bienseance me le permet, je faicts icy sentir mes inclinations et affections; mais plus librement et plus volontiers le faits-je de bouche à quiconque desire en estre informé. Tant y a qu'en ces memoires, si on y regarde, on trouvera que j'ay tout dict, ou tout designé. Ce que je ne puis exprimer, je le montre au doigt." (III 9 983 B)

With respect to language we know that Montaigne finds both the vocabulary and the usage inadequate. He wishes to avoid the word which attracts too much attention to itself. As his ideas become more personal, Montaigne invents new words or phrases to express ideas and feelings which have not been expressed before. As Starobinski points out, he employs a "...langage prodigieusement actif."[20]

In addition, he uses humor to whet the reader's interest, to provide a kind of comic relief for some of his more serious pronouncements. As Gray states, "Le comique de Montaigne appartient à cette dernière catégorie [celui que le langage crée]; il faut même y regarder d'assez près pour le surprendre en train de s'épanouir. Il doit ce qu'il est à la structure de la phrase ou au choix des mots et pas à certaines distractions particulières des hommes ou des événements."[21] Often Montaigne uses particular words such as "plaisant," "ridicule," and "se moquer" in telling a story. These thus serve as signposts to the humorous elements in his style. At times, he sees himself and others in a humorous light, and he often catches himself in the act of taking himself seriously. In so doing, he turns his humor upon himself. Although the intent of Montaigne's work is serious, humor is present and plays an important role in provoking and sustaining his reader's interest. Since the *Essais* are in essence a portrait of a man, we can see him smiling wryly at his own foibles and those of humanity in general. In essence, then, in treating the humorous elements of his style, we must recognize that Montaigne uses humor in its various manifestations not only for the sake "...of increasing the appeal of the *Essais*,"[22] but also because it is a basic part of his character and attitude toward life.

But the humor employed in the *Essais* is only one aspect of his style, and certainly Montaigne has been accused often enough of certain stylistic flaws. Chiefly, critics have quarreled concerning order in the *Essais*. In general most agree that an order is present albeit an individual and somewhat unusual one. Butor, for example, finds an order which is present when the work is looked at in its entirety. Ideas which appear to be presented in a disorderly fashion are in fact connected and developed when the work is viewed as one complete entity. For, as Gray has stated, "Il n'y a pas d'ordre chez lui dans le sens accepté du mot; il ne compose pas ses 'fantaisies', il les expose."[23] Gray finds in the work a unity which stems from Montaigne's portrayal of himself, and any unity present is a result of this self-portrait. In effect, Frame poses a similar thesis concerning the ordering of the *Essais*: "His order need not be logical; it must be that of his mind....For the style must be part of the man and of his portrait."[24] And Hatzfeld calls Montaigne's style that of "...studiata negligenza."[25] Because of this seeming carelessness, "...it takes experience and a rather keen eye for ideas and metaphors to see at an early reading the unity of many of Montaigne's essays."[26]

Perhaps Parslow gives the most extensive analysis of Montaigne's stylistic order when speaking of the composition of the *Essais*. Specifically, he states the following:

> Montaigne makes his theme a point of reference to which he repeatedly returns only to start off again in a new direction. The typical, simple trajectory of Montaigne's thought begins with an idea, moves about it in loosely articulated steps by a series of antitheses, references, and qualifications, and then returns. The thought seems to be advancing: however, it does not progress in a straight line but only out and around until its élan is exhausted and it drops back. In this way the

> central idea is illuminated from several disparate points of view.[27]

This passage bears out Traeger's thesis that there is an inner order and logic in Montaigne's writing, although it gives the appearance of being haphazard and random.

This study of Montaigne's work leads me to believe that order prevails. But, since this order is subject to the workings of a complex mind interested in and involved with many ideas at the same time, it may not be immediately discernible. The mortar exists, but it is tempered in the mold of Montaigne's character and personality. The point of the intellectual endeavor is to attempt some truth about the self. Only through truth, Montaigne thinks, does one approach value, that is—only after the arrival of truth, which is a continuing process, can one have the material for ethical action. That continuing process is effected by a dialectical movement between self and world. That dialectical movement is Montaigne's art—a purposeful intellectual process founded in his definition of truth's relative nature, which has to do with the absence of stasis in life. Essentially, moving dialectically between himself and the world, altering and being altered, his ideas are in an unceasing state of flux. What we see in the *Essais* is the portrait of a man ever thinking, feeling, living, and evolving. This exchange constitutes, in my opinion, the intellectual integrant of ordering.

Certainly Montaigne could have imposed an exterior order in the *Essais*, but "...Montaigne did not want to systematize his meditations after the fact; because to have done so would have been to destroy the very thing he was intent on preserving: the movement of his mind in the act of thinking with all its hesitations, erratic gropings, false steps, and sudden starts of insight."[28] As a consequence, Montaigne develops his own rhetoric to suit his purpose in the *Essais*.

Basically, examples serve to render his writing more meaningful from a phenomenological point of view. The stories he inserts in the *Essais* are not necessarily true, for as he himself states: "Aussi en l'estude que je traitte de noz moeurs et mouvements, les tesmoignages fabuleux, pourveu qu'ils soient possibles, y servent comme les vrais. Advenu ou non advenu, à Paris ou à Rome, à Jean ou à Pierre, c'est tousjours un tour de l'humaine capacité, duquel je suis utilement advisé par ce recit. Je le voy et en fay mon profit egalement en umbre qu'en corps." (I 21 105 C) Montaigne uses language to communicate "...un 'message' idéologique ou littéraire, et ne cherchant pas à prouver une vérité certaine mais une vérité relative, il nous communique cette vérité par une forme rhétorique dont la fonction est de montrer non pas qu'une chose est sûre, mais qu'elle est possible. De cette façon il concilie ses idées (sa façon de voir le monde) avec la forme qui les exprime, le signifié et le signifiant."[29] Ehrlich further contends that "...ce qui paraît être la peinture du moi est en réalité un véhicule qui fait partie d'un dessein bien plus vaste que parler de soi. It sert à démasquer, à corriger les abus et à faire la critique de son siècle. Nous verrons que ces réflexions convergent pour nous guider vers un thème fondamental de son oeuvre 'ôter les masques.'"[30]

The Tone of Self-Revelation

But, desirous as Montaigne is that obstacles to communication be eliminated, it is ironic that he, wishing to unmask a century, is, himself, accused of wearing a mask, of deliberately distorting the truth concerning himself, his work, his attitudes toward his life, and his relationship with others. In studying Montaigne's work we find statements which are apparently and almost blatantly untrue; for he frequently makes statements which are in opposition with his philosophy and use of language. His choice of language and his style are made up of "...ambiguity, irony, paradox, and contradiction...."[31] The presence of such elements gives rise to conflicting critical viewpoints concerning Montaigne's intention in a particular passage.

But the very fact that it is sometimes difficult to judge whether Montaigne is speaking honestly or seriously of himself and his work makes him appear more human, which is after all an object of the *Essais*.

As was said in the first section of this chapter, Montaigne emerges from his work as a sociable man, one who enjoys the company of others and seeks out capable and intelligent individuals with whom to converse: "C'est, à le bien prendre, de nos formes la plus rare, et forme qui se doit principallement à la nature. La fin de ce commerce, c'est simplement la privauté, frequentation et conference: l'exercice des ames, sans autre fruit." (III 3 824 B) In addition, he claims that his soul rejects lying. In point of fact, he says: "Mon ame, de sa complexion, refuit la menterie et hait mesmes à la penser." (II 18 648 C) And again: "Or, de moy, j'ayme mieux estre importun et indiscret que flateur et dissimulé." (II 17 649 A) Moreover, he links the subjects of lying and conversation in the following statement, remarkable, moreover, in its metaphoric brilliance: "Je festoye et caresse la verité en quelque main que je la trouve, et m'y rends alaigrement, et luy tends mes armes vaincues, de loing que je la vois approcher." (III 8 824 B) He also believes that people should accommodate themselves to the social level of the individuals with whom they are conversing: "Et le conseil de Platon ne me plaist pas, de parler tousjours d'un langage maestral à ses serviteurs, sans jeu, sans familiarité, soit envers les masles, soit envers les femelles. Car, outre ma raison, il est inhumain et injuste de faire tant valoir cette telle quelle prerogative de la fortune; et les polices où il se souffre moins de disparité entre les valets et les maistres, me semblent les plus equitables." (III 3 822 C)

To limn some more strokes of the portrait, Montaigne claims that when he is engaged in an argument "...je suis parfaict en la souffrance, car j'endure la revenche, non seulement aspre, mais indiscrete aussi, sans alteration." (III 8 938 B) (Is he laughing at himself just a little?) Furthermore, he seeks out people who contradict him in disputes: "Quand on me contrarie, on esveille mon attention, non pas ma cholere; je m'avance vers celuy qui me contredit, qui m'instruit." (III 7 924 B) Similarly: "En fin, je reçois et advoue toutes sortes d'atteinctes qui sont de droict fil, pour foibles qu'elles soient, mais je suis par trop impatient de celles qui se donnent sans forme. Il me chaut peu de la matiere, et me sont les opinions unes, et la victoire du subject à peu près indifferent." (III 8 925 B) His statements about himself show us one aspect of his personality, and even in this—the picture of the outward, social individual—there are contradictions as well as statements which are perhaps ironic in intent.

Montaigne dismisses small talk: "Et d'autant que je sommeille en toute autre communication et que je n'y preste que l'escorce de mon attention, il m'advient souvent, en telle sorte de propos abatus et lâches, propos de contenance, de dire et respondre des songes et bestises indignes d'un enfant et ridicules, ou de me tenir obstiné en silence, plus ineptement encore et incivilement." (III 3 819-820 B) Basically, he does not enjoy participating in idle pleasantries and feels inadequate in that situation; in order to escape, he finds it necessary to retreat into himself, to eschew superficial conversation. Often he claims to hide in his library in order to renew himself and reestablish contact with his inner person. Thus: "C'est là mon siege. J'essaie à m'en rendre la domination pure, et à soustraire ce seul coin à la communauté et conjugale, et filiale, et civile. Par tout ailleurs je n'ay qu'une auctorité verbale: en essence, confuse. Miserable à mon gré, qui n'a chez soy où estre à soy, où se faire particulierement la cour, où se cacher!" (III 3 828 C) He feels that it is better to be alone than in boring company: "Mais il vaut mieux encore estre seul qu'en compaignie ennuyeuse et inepte." (III 9 987 B) For nothing can be gained from those who have nothing to offer.

Modestly, Montaigne asserts that his friends credit him with some ability in correspondence: "Sur ce subject de lettres, je veux dire ce mot, que c'est un ouvrage auquel mes amys tiennent que je puis quelque chose." (I 40 252 B) Reflecting on his word he contends: "...mes discours sont, conforméement à mes meurs, bas et humbles." (III 13 1113 B) Such an utterance is seemingly yet another example of assumed meekness. In addition, he claims that he has an abominably poor memory: "C'est un outil de merveilleux service que la memoire, et sans lequel le jugement faict bien à peine son office: elle me manque du tout." (II 17 619 A)

The Defense of a Style

In many places throughout his work, Montaigne, well aware of the originality of his effort, attempts to justify the self-portrait, for example:

> Cette longue attention que j'employe à me considerer me dresse à juger aussi passablement des autres, et est peu de choses dequoy je parle plus heureusement et excusablement. Il m'advient souvant de voir et distinguer plus exactement les conditions de mes amys qu'ils ne font eux mesmes. J'en ay estonné quelqu'un par la pertinence de ma description, et l'ay adverty de soy. Pour m'estre, dès mon enfance, dressé à mirer ma vie dans celle d'autruy, j'ay acquis une complexion studieuse en cela, et, quand j'y pense, je laisse eschaper au tour de moy peu de choses qui y servent: contenances, humeurs, discours. (III 13 1076 B)

Earlier, he claims that it is only the mean-spirited who are afraid to speak well of themselves, for he says: "Cela m'a semblé aussi un peu lâche, qu'ayant eu à dire qu'il avoit exercé certain honorable magistrat à Romme, il s'aille excusant que ce n'est point par ostentation qu'il l'a dit. Ce traict me semble bas de poil pour une ame de sa sorte. Car le n'oser parler rondement de soy a quelque faute de coeur." (III 3 942 B) Although custom dictates that one never speak well of oneself, he dares to ignore it: "La coustume a faict le parler de soy vicieux, et le prohibe obstineement en hayne de la ventance qui semble tousjours estre attachée aux propres tesmoignages." (II 6 378 C)

In continuing his discussion of style, he forestalls criticism by admitting that he borrows from the Ancients, but he specifies thus:

> (A) Ainsi je ne pleuvy aucune certitude, si ce n'est de faire connoistre jusques à quel poinct monte, pour cette heure, la connoissance que j'en ay. Qu'on ne s'attende pas aux matieres, mais à la façon que j'y donne.
>
> (C) Qu'on voye, en ce que j'emprunte, si j'ay sçeu choisir de quoy rehausser mon propos. Car je fay dire aux autres ce que je ne puis bien dire, tantost par foiblesse de mon langage, tantost par foiblesse de mon sens. Je ne compte pas mes emprunts, je les poise. Et si je les eusse voulu faire valoir par nombre, je m'en fusse chargé deux fois autant. Ils sont tous, ou fort peu s'en faut, de noms si fameux et anciens qu'ils me semblent se nommer assez sans moi. (II 10 408)

So it is that he perpetuates and renews classical literature, endowing it with a fresh context. From the broad treatment of the style of self-revelation, we can now move to his comments on language evoking the mask and the self-portrait.

The Validity of the Self-Portrait: Montaigne and the Critics

Montaigne states that there is nothing to be gained by hiding behind a false face, for: "Si vous estes couard et qu'on vous honnore pour un vaillant homme, est-ce de vous qu'on parle? on vous prend pour un autre." (III 5 847 C) He continues with a discussion of disguises and the many forms they take. For example, he cites the custom of keeping secret the troubles of marriage from fear of losing face with others: "Les aigreurs comme les douceurs du mariage se tiennent secrettes par les sages. Et, parmy les autres importunes conditions qui se trouvent en iceluy, cette cy, à un homme langagier comme je suis, est des principales: que la coustume rend indecent et nuisible qu'on communique à persone[*sic*] tout ce qu'on en sçait et qu'on en sent." (III 5 870 C) He further submits that names and reputations are totally unimportant, particularly when we consider that we are all moving towards death: (A) "Moy, je tiens que je ne suis que chez moy; et, de cette autre mienne vie qui loge en la connoissance de mes amis, (C) à la considerer nue et simplement en soy, (A) je sçay bien que je n'en sens fruict ny jouyssance que par la vanité d'une opinion fantastique. Et, quand je seray mort, je m'en resentiray encores beaucoup moins...." (II 16 626)

From this point, we can proceed to the consideration of the validity of the self-portrait, upon which Montaigne himself moreover casts doubt:

> (B) Moy qui suis Roy de la matiere que je traicte, et qui n'en dois conte à personne, ne m'en crois pourtant pas du tout: je hasarde souvent des boutades de mon esprit, desquelles je me deffie, (C) et certaines finesses verbales, dequoy je secoue les oreilles; (B) mais je les laisse courir à l'avanture. (C) Je voys qu'on s'honore de pareilles choses. Ce n'est pas à moy seul d'en juger. Je me presente debout et couché, le devant et le derriere, à droite et à gauche, et en tous mes naturels plis. (B) Les esprits, voire pareils en force, ne sont pas tousjours pareils en application et en goust. (III 8 943)

The following contradictory passages in turn similarly cast doubt on the validity of the self-portrait. For example, he contends that he reveals himself completely throughout his writing: "Je ne laisse rien à desirer et deviner de moy....Je reviendrois volontiers de l'autre monde pour démentir celuy qui me formeroit autre que je n'estois, fut ce pour m'honorer." (III 9 983 B) On the other hand, he sometimes hesitates to reveal himself so unreservedly because he believes such disclosure renders him vulnerable: "Des vivans mesmes, je sens qu'on parle tousjours autrement qu'ils ne sont. Et si à toute force je n'eusse maintenu un amy que j'ay perdu, on me l'eust deschiré en mille contraires visages." (III 9 983 B) Again, he claims elsewhere that others can come to know him in all aspects through his writing: "Tant y a qu'en ces memoires, si on y regarde, on trouvera que j'ay tout dict, ou tout designé." (III 9 983 B) He subsequently claims: "Joint qu'à adventure ay-je quelque obligation particuliere à ne dire qu'à demy, à dire confusément, à dire discordamment." (III 9 995-996 C) He continues, stating: "...je promets volontiers un peu moins de ce que je puis et de ce que j'espere tenir." (III 10 1024 B) In light then of the description of the various qualities applicable to him, it is ironic to consider that Montaigne perceives his self-portrait as a complete entity in which, as partially cited above: "Tant y a qu'en ces memoires, si on y regarde, on trouvera que j'ay tout dict, ou tout designé. Ce que je ne puis exprimer, je le montre au doigt:

Verum animo satis haec vestigia parva sagaci
Sunt, per quae possis cognoscere caetera tute." (III 9 983 B)

Therefore, as further seen above, he does not wish people to continue debating his genuine identity: "Je reviendrois volontiers de l'autre monde pour démentir celuy qui me formeroit autre que je n'estois, fut ce pour m'honorer." (III 9 983 B) However, the debate occasioned by the self-portrait and Montaigne's treatment of the mask still rages, and it might be said that the very richness, variety, and humor of Montaigne's writing have contributed to this prolonged dissection of his work and character.

We are left with Montaigne's words and with the many critical interpretations of those words. How much of Montaigne's self-depreciation is to be believed? To what degree does he intend to be taken seriously? Thibaudet accepts Montaigne's self-portrayal as essentially serious: "Ce n'est que son portrait que Montaigne nous a donné."[32] Thibaudet believes that Montaigne presents himself according to his own true evaluation of himself, and although we may disagree with Montaigne's self-evaluation, what we encounter in the *Essais* is the image Montaigne beholds when he contemplates himself: "Il s'agit de nous faire *voir* notre interlocuteur, mais de le faire voir en tous temps et tous lieux....Ce style nous permet d'aller par-delà le signe au mot prononcé, puis au mouvement, puis à tout l'être."[33] Regosin agrees, stating: "The words become fixed as the man is portrayed and, we understand, the man assumes being through the words."[34] Furthermore, Regosin claims that "The distance between the writer-observer and self acting...is closed."[35] Hallie concurs with this interpretation, stating that "...Montaigne is not presenting a mold of the face that men artificially prepare to meet the faces that they meet. He is presenting a mold of his personality down to its guts."[36] And Conche claims that Montaigne's "...'contradictions' ne sont qu'apparentes: ou les mots ne sont pas pris dans le même sens, ou il ne juge pas du même point de vue— qu'il nous en avertisse ou non."[37] On the other hand, Lablénie assumes a somewhat different position, stating: "Il est vrai toutefois que des demi-silences, des affirmations confuses ou contradictoires lui sont imposées par une prudence, que la prudence lui interdit apparemment d'expliquer...."[38]

Other critics take a stand on this issue which is diametrically opposed to the ones presented above. By and large many critics feel as Moreau does:

"...Montaigne nous laisse dans le doute sur ses idées véritables; nous ne savons jamais s'il dit vrai ou s'il sourit."[39] In addition to agreeing with Moreau about the humor in the self-portrait, Nolan goes somewhat beyond, suggesting that since Montaigne does not want to "...appear over-confident, it is only natural for him to appear to have reservations about his ability."[40] Moreover, "...by presenting the laughable along with the laudable..."[41] side of himself, Montaigne feels that he will more easily gain the sympathy of the reader.

Supporting this interpretation, Traeger says, "Die Äußerungen über die eigene Unordnung scheinen zumindest ebenso ambivalent wie die ironische Bescheidenheit, mit der Montaigne allgemein seine Selbstdarstellungen würzt."[42] Basically, Traeger states that Montaigne is consciously and deliberately self-deprecatory: "Ausdrücke wie die von uns unterstrichenen—'extravagant', 'folie', 'fantastique', (das letzte oft mit 'vain', 'vanité' gepaart)—erscheinen in den Essais ambivalent: bald abwertend, bald als halbironische Floskeln einer Bescheidenheit, die bewußt ist, nicht ernstgenommen werden zu können."[43] Montaigne is often thus thought to be merely defending "...seine menschliche Einstellung...mit einem Argument, das ersichtlich nicht bestimmt ist, wörtlich genommen zu werden."[44] In carrying this idea still further, Traeger arrives at a scale of values which he assigns to Montaigne. He claims that the following scheme summarizes Montaigne's implied beliefs: "Montaigne verachtet die menschliche Neigung, das Urteil dem Wunsch zu beugen. Selbstüberschätzung also würde ihn zur Selbstmißachtung zwingen. Das Urteil dagegen, das sich unbestechlich gegen das eigene Ich richtet, gelangt zwar zu etwas, das einer Selbstverringerung ähnelt, aber es erweist dabei seine Schärfe und somit einen wesentlichen Wert des Ich. Wir erhalten ein Schema dieser Art:

Selbstverringerung=Urteilsschärfe⇒Selbstachtung

Selbstüberschätzung=Urteilstrübung⇒Selbstmißachtung"[45]

Ehrlich also argues with this interpretation, but she makes the following qualification: "Le masque est une expression de la mauvaise foi, du mensonge, de la manipulation intéressée; le 'jeu' fait partie de la condition humaine générale, de la condition de celui même qui ne triche point."[46] She holds that certain aspects of Montaigne's self-portrait fall into the category of game rather than mask. However, it does seem that the distinction she makes is merely a verbal one. She continues: "...le 'jeu' au niveau réel est transfiguré en 'jeu' au niveau fictif et c'est dans cette perspective-là que l'on aperçoit la signification du portrait. Il fait partie de la structure générale de l'oeuvre."[47]

Yet another critic, Parslow, takes a similar stand, feeling that self-depreciation is a role which Montaigne assumes—that finally the *Essais* "...were his other self through which Montaigne came to discover and affirm his true identity."[48] Bowen also agrees, but she goes a step further in stating that "...Montaigne's style is much too well balanced, too intellectual, and too metaphorical to be unconscious, and his devaluation of it is analogous to his pretense of lack of moral commitment. A man who writes spontaneously, as he speaks, will be more endearing to the reader than a self-conscious rhetorician, so Montaigne will pretend to be that man...Montaigne is painting a literary portrait which is not intended to be taken at its face value."[49]

Frame's interpretation further supports these contentions. He states: "Self-portrayal makes a man arrange himself to appear in public; thus since Montaigne is constantly describing himself, he is constantly adorning himself."[50] In addition, Frame states: "A true portrait must change as the subject changes."[51] According to Frame, Montaigne fears the self-portrait would be thought presumptuous: "But most of the time he apparently feels that in order to be accepted as truthful he must be less truthful than modest."[52]

In evaluating these varied critical assessments of Montaigne's self-portrait and the extent of disguise or distortion in that portrayal, we should be aware that in any attempt to represent the flesh and bone of a man in words, difficulties arise and contradictions appear. Irony is indispensible in order to faithfully render man—flesh and bone, since truths of one age compared to those of another—or one day to the next—may result in paradox. Certainly, it seems most logical to assume that Montaigne is very well aware of the contradictions inherent in himself and in his portrait, but in his attempt to faithfully render himself with words, he can not exclude his own sense of humor and his penchant for self-irony. To a large extent, he is most faithful in portraying himself when, in an unexpected aside, he sketches witty and often ironic *aperçus* of himself. In this case Bowen's assertion that Montaigne's "...main intention is to jolt, disconcert, and amuse his reader...,"[53] must be taken into account, and it seems indeed incontrovertible that "A man who so often uses *mais* and *au contraire* is a man accustomed to seeing both, or all, sides of a question, who will exploit all the possibilities of existing paradoxes and then go on to create new ones."[54]

It is obvious, then, that contradictions do exist in Montaigne's portrait, that some are deliberate and that others arise from his evolving character. In the *Essais*, Montaigne exposes contemporary hypocrisies by virtue of the mask theme in which they are implicit. This wise indirection renders Montaigne himself less vulnerable. Furthermore, he sagely includes himself in the general reprobation.

In essence, one of his basic themes concerns the difficulty of bridging the gap between man's inner reality and that of the world, between what is and what appears to be, between reality and illusion. The mask, both his own and that of others, is only one aspect of the basic difficulty of human existence—the attempt to use language to rejoin the interior and exterior reality of man.

What is the relation between illusion and reality in Montaigne? How does the mask theme in his language connect them or does it? Language, as an attempt to rejoin the interior and exterior reality of man, suggests philosophical implications. Language is an instrument of the reason, a tool, a vehicle of the mind. The mind, the reason, is the tragic faculty of man. That is, it distinguishes him from the rest of the world, from subjective union with the natural. Montaigne says man may once have been innocent (certain Indian tribes may be still) but is no longer—certainly a reference to the "Machiavellian" environment of his period. This implies a conception of the increasing sophistication of the rational faculties...an increasing separation, an increasing perception of objectification of the world. This is the tragic view, of course; the only instrument which can unite man to the world is the very one which distinguishes him from it. Men may, however, *further* alienate themselves from other men by a purposeful obscuring of the self. The utilization of mask, of dissimulation is everywhere, and it is the essential human evil. Language can be used to join the interior and exterior reality of man. The mask makes that attempt at union more difficult. There is a possibility that union can never be attained, of course, but the attempt is the responsibility of intellect and ethics, and it may be the civilizing factor in life. Illusion is the mask and reality is a relative thing, whether under the mask or exposed, but illusion depends upon the reality which is a reflection of the *intention* of men, their motivation; we must know a man to know his intention. This is an intellectual endeavor. This is Montaigne's art.

The interior and exterior may once have been joined in a time of fewer masks—a time of innocence. Innocence, however, is not civilization; civilization is the removal of masks, the will to remove them. Montaigne thinks that the gap between illusion and reality has widened. There is, consequently, an urgency to his view.

Many comment on the dissimulation, the Machiavellianism, of the time. But do any suggest such a dialectical use of language to mitigate the situation? Orthodoxies have obviously been unequal to the attack of secular humanism. The basis of Montaigne's resolution is in the intellectual method and in a philosophical skepticism. Since language is a reflection of reason, which is not necessarily ethical—it may not only serve to alienate, to manipulate, to barbarize; it may also serve to unite, to ameliorate, to civilize. It is unfortunately the primary *instrument* of reason, and its reflection of the duality of intention (toward union or separation, civilization or barbarism) is an accurate one. It can mask true intention; it can reveal truth. What are truth and illusion in this regard? Reality is true intention (good or ill) and is definable in terms of action or more abstractly form; it is the totality of relative truth, reflective of the organic and therefore changing nature of the natural, the unreasonable, as well as the changing nature of the living reason and its impulsion toward self and others. Mask is illusion; it attempts to hide truth. And truth *is* definable in a limited as well as a more expanded, though hardly metaphysical or absolute or ideal sense for Montaigne. Man acts; action is not possible without choice, without decision. An act therefore is true, or at least the intention is truth. The "act" may be illusion—a concoction to misrepresent the *decision*. Words can only unite illusion and reality of *action*—if one is aware of the precision of their applicability to the ambiguity of intention and motivation. The associations of words, their history of changing meaning, lend them to misappropriation or distortion, if not outright abuse. It is the responsibility of ethical man, of civilized persons, *to understand the potential of language*, if not necessarily for ethical use then for defensive action. But language can not be separated from men, from reason. Therefore it becomes the responsibility of men to inquire after knowledge and the nature of knowledge.

Montaigne's conception of language has, consequently, an epistemological foundation. What is knowledge and what kind of knowledge is obtainable? And how is this related to a definition of the reason, of the mind? *What* can be known? These questions depend also upon one's perception of life, the distinction between body and mind, nature and reason, and the participation of the reason in the organic: its definition is a *living* entity itself, incapable of stasis.

Montaigne's conception is obviously skeptical in its attempt to *define only* contingent reality. The *reason* can know no other and the world of action is apparently (and this is a significant appearance) dependent upon mind, not the metaphysical.

His intellectual method is emphatic in its dependence upon a definition of the relativity of truth and the duality of intention. Knowing truth is a *process*, as is living; but it *can* proceed along rational lines.

The self-portrait represents a dialogue with the self as well as a revelation to the world.

Both processes are necessary to a definition of truth and finally—ethical action. If one can not distinguish between illusion and reality, one can not determine the ethical or the good. So, its *essential* separateness from *all* else, its definition of the being, and the nature of its relation to the world are a necessary prelude to any intellectual understanding of the self or of the world or of the nature of truth.

Montaigne's dialectical method is a reflection of his conception of truth, of course. The only approach to it is of a dialectical sort. A state of flux becomes an intellectual integrant of ordering.

Metaphors for Language and Man

Certainly, much has been made of Montaigne's statement that he wishes to create words "...de chair et d'os...," (III 5 977) but any study of the *Essais* shows that this metaphor, which likens the human body to words, recurs frequently. For example, Montaigne speaks of shaping words into sentences and molding them into a body: "On nous tient quatre ou cinq ans à entendre les mots et les coudre en clauses; encores autant à en proportionner un grand corps, estendu en quatre ou cinq parties, et autres cinq, pour le moins, à les sçavoir brefvement mesler et entrelasser de quelque subtile façon." (I 26 168 A) Again, he writes: "De cent membres et visages qu'a chaque chose, j'en prens un tantost à lecher seulement, tantost à effleurer; et par fois à pincer jusqu'à l'os. J'y donne une poincte, non pas le plus largement, mais le plus profondement que je sçay." (I 50 302 A) And in an extended metaphor, he speaks of the "...SKELETOS où, d'une veuë, les veines, les tendons paroissent, chaque piece en son siege." (II 6 379 C) Elsewhere he uses the image of the digestive system of the human body with reference to words: "Ce sont icy, un peu plus civilement, des excremens d'un vieil esprit, dur tantost, tantost lache et tousjours indigeste." (III 9 946 B) There likewise occur numerous other instances, among which the following: "C'est tesmoignage de crudité et indigestion que de regorger la viande comme on l'a avallée. L'estomac n'a pas faict son operation, s'il n'a faict changer la façon et la forme à ce qu'on luy avoit donné à cuire." (I 26 151 A); "Ceux qui ont le corps gresle, le grossissent d'embourrures: ceux qui ont la matiere exile, l'enflent de paroles." (I 26 157 C); "...tantost il luy en donnera la moelle et la substance toute maschée." (I 26 160 A); "Ce sont là preceptes espineux et mal plaisans, de ces mots vains et descharnez, où il n'y a point de prise, rien qui vous esveille l'esprit. En cette cy l'ame trouve où mordre et où se paistre. Ce fruict est plus grand, sans comparaison, et si sera plutost meury." (I 26 160 A); "...incapable de prendre la viande plus massive et plus ferme..." (I 26 170 A); "...encore ne sont ce pas lettres vuides et descharnées..." (I 40 252 A); "J'y viens tout preparé du logis: il ne me faut point d'alechement ny de sause: je menge bien la viande toute crue; et, au lieu de m'eguiser l'apetit par ces preparatoires et avant-jeux, on me le lasse et affadit." (II 10 414 A); "...ils veulent nous mascher les morceaux..." (II 10 417 A); "...je remache ces grands noms entre les dents et les faicts retenir à mes oreilles." (III 9 997 B).

As is readily apparent from the preceding catalog of quotations in which the words-as-flesh-and-bone metaphor appears, the image is one Montaigne enjoys using and which well fits his purpose. Such language is vital and unusual because it links the complexity of man's body with the convoluted workings of his mind and spirit. The end result is the word become flesh; hence the man and his century emerge in bold, emphatic relief.

Of course, there are several other major metaphors which Montaigne uses to depict the interior man, and of primary importance is the metaphor which deals with sewing, as for example: "Quand je l'appelle un badin, un veau, je n'entrepren pas de luy coudre à jamais ces tiltres; ny ne pense me desdire pour le nommer tantost honeste homme." (I 38 234 C); "Je tors bien plus volontiers une bonne sentence pour la coudre sur moy, que je ne tors mon fil pour l'aller querir." (I 26 171 C) Here he joins the foregoing with his flesh metaphor by mentioning seams in a fabric and comparing them to bones and veins in the human body: "La plus part des lecteurs, pour avoir trouvé une pareille robbe, pensent tresfaucement tenir un pareil corps. La force et les nerfs ne s'empruntent point; les atours et le manteau s'emprunte." (I 26 172 C) He states further: "Le remuement d'une seule syllabe meslera nos fusées...." (II 16 627 A) In still another metaphor Montaigne deals with a comparison of words and seeds: "Si suis je trompé, si guere d'autres donnent plus à prendre en la matiere, et, comment que ce soit, mal ou bien, si nul escrivain l'a semée ny guere plus materielle ny au moins plus drue en son papier." (I 40 251 C) And again: "(A) Une bonne institution, elle change le jugement et les meurs, comme il advint à Polemon, ce jeune homme Grec debauché, qui, estant allé ouïr par rencontre une leçon de (C) Xenocrates, (A) ne remerqua pas seulement l'eloquence et la suffisance du lecteur, et n'en rapporta pas seulement en la maison la science de quelque belle matiere, mais un fruit plus apparent et plus solide, qui fut le soudain changement et amendement de sa premiere vie." (II 17 660)

Another important metaphor which enriches Montaigne's style deals with travel. He often speaks of the journey into the self through words and conversation, and a general theme which runs through all his work concerns itself with this journey into self-knowledge through conversation with others. In effect, he often criticizes language because it is inadequate to an expression of all human feelings and thoughts, and in "De l'institution des enfans," he speaks of "...des mots vains et deschamez...," (I 26 160 A) and of the "...si sots, qui se destournent de leur voye un quart de lieuë, pour courir apres un beau mot...." (I 26 171 A) Often when he employs this metaphor as he does particularly in "De la vanité," and in the "Apologie," he uses the metaphor of soldiers and war to depict the bold, strong, and simple actions and use of words: indeed, such is the language he utilizes in the *Essais*.

The metaphor is a bridge between life and words. Why is the organic metaphor peculiar and relevant to the artistic and intellectual method? Montaigne wants organic metaphors for life and for language which is a reflection of life. The word is not the thing. Words approach reality or illusion, but since they are by their nature nearer to illusion, words reflect an inherently tragic truth.

The role of metaphor for Montaigne is dependent upon the referent, upon what is to be spoken of figuratively. The realities he envisions—the realities of the internal (the mind), the external (the natural world including humanity, of course), and the metaphysical or the inscrutable—determine the type of metaphor used. For the living, he prefers organic metaphor; for the inscrutable, the imprecise. But since his perspective is primarily of this world, it is organic metaphor which most satisfactorily relates words to life, bridges the gap between them, for both words and life are reflective of the changing (organic) nature of the totality of what man and the world are. Abstraction is not easily relatable to the nature of the flux of the mind or the body, which operate in the precision of the momentary, though it may be the only satisfactory sort of metaphor which Montaigne thinks is best undescribed, which is really indescribable.

The organic metaphor is appropriate, of course, not only to man, but to language itself, his reflection. Metaphors for language which liken it to the body link the body and the world to reason via its vehicle, words. So as reason bridges the gap (*can* bridge it), so do words and some words better than others, it would seem.

Montaigne, humanist, imposes upon man the burden of decision in the ethical sphere, for the faculty of reason is not necessarily ethical, of course. And this burden is operable everywhere, for to live is to be presented with choices, not the least of which is the choice of the word, the use of language. Language is as potent as the mind, and its use becomes an ethical or moral issue. Metaphor may bridge the gap between words and life. But there is no literal bridge from the reason to the world—there is only the *attempt* to organize, an attempt in which there is inherent weakness: the imprecise describes the imprecise. But the approach of the two may momentarily be close enough to occasion society and moral action or the uncivilized and the destructive. So there are two problematic areas—one more philosophical, one less so: the essential relationship of the mind to the world and the ethical decisions occasioned by that always inscrutable but continually recurring union/approach. The miracle is that the mind can effect any union with the world, but the extent of its approach to union is the world of men as we know it.

Montaigne's concern is not so much with this tragic affair, but rather with its effect—the world of men in action and the ethical application of language in particular.

The Potency of Language: Depicting Exterior Reality

Language and the Reflection of Life

If through figurative language Montaigne attempts to portray the interior world—in the relationship or rather lack of relationship which he sees between language and life, he is attempting to reveal the difficulty inherent in man's efforts to depict exterior life through language. The relation between words and deeds becomes a central concern. Montaigne well understands the potency of language, the fact that words advance both good and evil causes—indeed, that man need be aware of the enormous power of words to identify or distort reality: "He is a Humanist profoundly aware of the deep relationship between one's language and one's life."[55] He believes that language expresses life but that it also may alter it. People attempt to represent behavior and actions through words; however, language is often inadequate to express life with all its contradictions. Despite this, Montaigne sets himself the task of attempting to capture life in general and his own life in particular in language. The contradictions which he finds in life and in himself must be reflected in language.

Montaigne is only too well aware of the difficulty of making the leap between thought and language as he states twice in the "Apologie": "Je voy les philosophes Pyrrhoniens qui ne peuvent exprimer leur generale conception en aucune maniere de parler: car il leur faudroit un nouveau langage." (II 12 527 A) "Quand nous disons que l'infinité des siecles tant passez qu'avenir, n'est à Dieu qu'un instant; que sa bonté, sapience, puissance sont mesme chose avecques son essence, nostre parole le dict, mais nostre intelligence ne l'apprehende point." (II 12 528 A) He develops this idea further when he speaks of the names which are applied to things. They do not alter the essential reality of the thing named, but they represent man's attempt to categorize the corporeal and incorporeal in his life: "Nous sommes tous creux et vuides: ce n'est pas de vent et de voix que nous avons à nous remplir; il nous faut de la substance plus solide à nous reparer." (II 16 618 A) Finally, this consciousness leads him to the pronouncement that although language affects life, as illustrated by the following account:

> J'y ay aussi remarqué cela, qu'il fait grand cas de ses exhortations aux soldats avant le combat: car, où il veut montrer avoir esté surpris ou pressé, il allegue tousjours cela, qu'il n'eust pas seulement loysir de haranguer son armée. Avant cette grande bataille contre ceux de Tournay: Caesar, dict-il, ayant ordonné du reste, courut soudainement où la fortune le porta, pour enhorter ses gens; et rencontrant la dixiesme legion, il n'eust loisir de leur dire, sinon qu'ils eussent souvenance de leur vertu accoustumée, qu'ils ne s'estonnassent point et soustinsent hardiment l'effort des adversaires; et par ce que l'ennemy estoit des-jà approché à un jet de trait, il donna le signe de la bataille; et de là estant passé soudainement ailleurs pour en encourager d'autres, il trouva qu'ils estoyent desjà aux prises. Voylà ce qu'il en dict en ce lieu là. De vray, sa langue luy a fait en plusieurs lieux de bien notables services; et estoit, de son temps mesme, son eloquence militaire en telle recommendation que plusieurs en son armée recueilloyent ses harangues; et par ce moyen il en fut assemblé des volumes qui ont duré long temps apres luy. Son parler avoit des graces particulieres, si que ses familiers, et, entre autres, Auguste, oyant reciter ce qui en avoit esté recueilli, reconnoissoit jusques aux phrases et aux mots ce qui n'estoit pas du sien. (II 34 738 A)

indeed, has a life of its own, it is likewise true that often words and acts are at variance. Montaigne further advances that "La vie est un nouvement materiel et corporel, action imparfaicte de sa propre essence, et desreglée; je m'emploie à la servir selon elle." (III 9 988 B) And also: "Les hommes vont ainsin. On laisse les loix et preceptes suivre leur voie, nous en tenons une autre; non par desreiglement de meurs seulement mais par opinion souvent et par jugement contraire. Sentez lire un discours de philosophie: l'invention, l'eloquence, la pertinence frape incontinent vostre esprit et vous esmeut; il n'y a rien qui chatouille ou poigne vostre conscience; ce n'est pas à elle qu'on parle, est-il pas vray?" (III 9 989 C) Often he uses the concept concerning the connection between words and deeds, a Ciceronian topos, in a pejorative sense, as when he relates the following anecdotes: "Et quoy cet autre? Les Atheniens estoyent à choisir de deux architectes, à conduire une grande fabrique. Le premier, plus affeté, se presenta avec un beau discours premedité sur le subject de cette besongne, et tiroit le jugement du peuple à sa faveur. Mais l'autre, en trois mots: Seigneurs Atheniens, ce que cetuy a dict, je le feray." (I 26 170 B) "Si les gestes de Xenophon et de Caesar n'eussent de bien loing surpassé leur eloquence, je ne croy pas qu'ils les eussent jamais escris. Ils ont cherché à recommander non leur dire, mais leur faire." (I 40 249 A)

These, then, are topics which Montaigne treats in showing us the relationship between language and life, word and deed. As Ehrlich points out: "Montaigne ne croit pas à la concordance idéale de la chose et du mot."[56] He does, however, believe that man attempts to apply names to an inner reality, attempts to shape and control his world through language.

Education and Language: Toward a Truer Reflection of Life

Despite his pejorative statements concerning language and his cognizance of the difficulty of shaping language into a reflection of life, Montaigne feels that it can be done since certainly he himself attempts to mirror his life in words. In essence, Montaigne develops the ideal of a world in which people can be educated to become better individuals. As Tauro states: "Ma come non ammettere l'importanza di questa dottrina dell'educazione dello spirito che fa del linguaggio nè più nè meno che uno strumento del pensiero, un umile servo costretto a seguire e a servire la volontà e a rispecchiare fedelmente all'esterno, se non elegantemente, il mondo interiore di pensieri e d'immagini?"[57]

Indeed, Montaigne comes to espouse some very definite notions concerning education and the learning of foreign languages; his ideas are often compared with those of John Dewey: "...he anticipates his concern with the child as an entire person and with his active participation in his own education—with learning by doing and the lessons of things, not only of books. He has many affinities with the modern theories—in their unadulterated form—of John Dewey."[58] Montaigne thinks that books are not nearly so important as experience in learning and that children learn much more from participating in life than from book learning.

Certainly, Montaigne's ideas owe their formation to his own educational experience. Also, his father's attitude toward the education of children is a decisive factor in shaping Montaigne's pedagogical philosophy.

As is well known, Montaigne was taught Latin by hearing only it spoken from infancy. He later approves this as an ideal method by which to teach a child a language. He claims that when children are taught a foreign language, they ought to be taught when they are very young by being made to speak that language: "Je voudrois qu'on commençast à le promener des sa tendre enfance, et premierement, pour faire d'une pierre deux coups, par les nations voisines où le langage est plus esloigné du nostre, et auquel, si vous ne la formez de bon'heure, la langue ne se peut plier." (I 26 153 A) Emphasizing the importance of speaking the language and that of rote memorization of declensions, he comments further on the learning of Greek and Latin: "...mes precepteurs domestiques, m'ont dict souvent que j'avois ce langage, en mon enfance, si prest et si à main, qu'ils craingnoient à m'accoster." (I 26 174 A) This idea also tallies with his own education inasmuch as his father has him taught Greek "...par forme d'ébat et d'exercice." (I 26 174 A) Montaigne comments that upon being sent to school, he loses most of his ability to speak Latin and that the school, rather than helping, hinders his true education: "Mon Latin s'abastardit incontinent, duquel depuis par desacoustumance j'ay perdu tout usage. Et ne me servit cette mienne nouvelle institution que de me faire enjamber d'arrivée aux premieres classes: car, à treize ans que je sortis du college, j'avoy achevé mon cours (qu'ils appellent), et à la verité sans aucun fruit que je peusse à present mettre en compte." (I 26 175 A)

Montaigne thus criticizes the study of Greek and Latin as it was currently conducted in schools. He maintains that people, through the study of the classical tongues, are led to feel learned when in fact they are not: "(A) Qu'il ne luy demande pas seulement compte des mots de sa leçon, mais du sens et de la substance, et qu'il juge du profit qu'il aura fait, non par le tesmoignage de sa memoire, mais de sa vie. Que ce qu'il viendra d'apprendre, il le lui face mettre en cent visages et accommoder à autant de divers subjets, pour voir s'il l'a encore bien pris et bien faict sien, (C) prenant l'instruction de son progrez des paedagogismes de Platon. (A) C'est tesmoignage de crudité et indigestion que de regorger la viande comme on l'a avallée." (I 26 151), for, according to Montaigne, true learning is achieved only when a man is able to read others' writings through the lens of his own mind's eye. Montaigne holds: "Pour revenir à mon propos, il n'y a tel que d'allécher l'appétit et l'affection, autrement on ne faict que des asnes chargez de livres. On leur donne à coups de foüet en garde leur pochette pleine de science, laquelle, pour bien faire, il ne faut pas seulement loger chez soy, il la faut espouser." (I 26 177 A)

> Un tale sistema di educazione il Montaigne ritiene che sia più adatto a pervertire lo spirito umano che a rettamente formarlo; ed ai cattivi effetti del sistema di educazione prevalente nei suoi tempi, preferisce l'assenza di particolare educazione, o, come ora si direbbe, l'educazione naturale di quelle persone che, per la loro speciale condizione, tengono il più umile posto nella gerarchia sociale, cioè i contadini e gli umili lavoratori della terra, i quali, non avendo avuto una specifica educazione linguistica, guardano più alle cose che alle parole e trovano sempre le parole opportune per indicare le cose.[59]

In fact, Montaigne states that "J'aymeroy mieux que mon fils apprint aux tavernes à parler, qu'aux escholes de la parlerie," (III 8 926-927 B) because the simple common speech is franker and more honest.

In summary, we may conclude that Montaigne advocates teaching the child to use language as a tool for expressing his ideas clearly and simply. He does not want to teach words or subjects; rather he wants to teach people—people who can learn from experience, who can absorb and rework ideas, not merely parrot them.

The Abuse of Language: Professional Idioms and the Distortion of Reality

Montaigne's attitudes on the various types of language are an extension of his educational philosophy. That which is natural, sincere, and clear is praised; that which is obscure, devious, and unnatural is disparaged and satirized. On the whole, he attacks doctors, lawyers, judges, courtiers, and pedants for abandoning simple, natural speech in order to deceive themselves or others.

He discusses the idioms of the specific professions while pointing out the various abuses perpetrated against the language:

> (C) Le vieil Dionysius estoit tres grand chef de guerre, comme il convenait à sa fortune; mais il se travailloit à donner principale recommendation de soy par la poësie, et si n'y sçavoit rien. (A) *Optat ephippia bos piger, optat arare caballus.* (C)Par ce train vous ne faictes jamais rien qui vaille. (A) Ainsin, il faut rejetter tousjours l'architecte, le peintre, le cordonnier, et ainsi du reste, chacun à son gibier. Et, à ce propos, à la lecture des histoires, qui est le subjet de toutes gens, j'ay accoustumé de considerer qui en sont les escrivains: si ce sont personnes qui ne facent autre profession que de lettres, j'en apren principalement le stile et le langage; si ce sont medecins, je les croy plus volontiers en ce qu'ils

> nous disent de la temperature de l'air, de la santé et complexion des Princes, des blessures et maladies; si Jurisconsultes, il en faut prendre les controverses des droicts, les loix, l'establissement des polices et choses pareilles; si Theologiens, les affaires de l'Eglise, censures Ecclesiastiques, dispenses et mariages; si courtisans, les meurs et les ceremonies; si gens de guerre, ce qui est de leur charge, et principalement les deductions des exploits, où ils se sont trouvez en personne; si Ambassadeurs, les menées, intelligences et practiques, et maniere de les conduire. (I 17 72-73)

In particular, doctors came under censure for their misuse of the language. Montaigne describes rhetorical interference in language in the following example: "Melanthius interrogé ce qu'il luy sembloit de la tragedie de Dionysius: Je ne l'ay, dict-il, point veuë, tant elle est offusquée de langage. Aussi la pluspart de ceux qui jugent les discours des grands debvroient dire: Je n'ay point entendu son propos, tant il estoit offusqué de gravité, de grandeur et de majesté." (III 8 935 B) Montaigne criticizes medical terminology and submits his own remedy as follows: "Je represente mes maladies, pour le plus, telles qu'elles sont, et evite les parolles de mauvais prognostique et exclamations composées. Sinon l'allegresse, aumoins la contenance rassise des assistans est propre pres d'un sage malade." (III 9 979 B) Furthermore, he decries medical prognoses, in particular the one addressed to him, which threatens him with pain and imminent death:

> Je consulte peu des alterations que je sens, car ces gens icy sont avantageux quand ils vous tiennent à leur misericorde: ils vous gourmandent les oreilles de leurs prognostiques; et, me surprenant autre fois affoibly du mal, m'ont injurieusement traicté de leurs dogmes et troigne magistrale, me menassant tantost de grandes douleurs, tantost de mort prochaine. Je n'en estois abbatu ny deslogé de ma place, mais j'en estois heurté et poussé; si mon jugement n'en est ny changé ny troublé, au moins il en estoit empesché; c'est tousjours agitation et combat. (III 13 1090 B)

Often Montaigne's comments concerning doctors are ironic or humorous, and they may reveal that Montaigne feels a personal distrust of them.

Other tongues which feel the prick of Montaigne's quill are those of lawyers. Montaigne castigates the legal parlance as being deliberately of obscure and/or ambiguous interpretation. He speaks further of lawyers and other professionals and comments on their use of language: "La part de l'Advocat est plus dificile que celle du Prescheur, et nous trouvons pourtant, ce m'est advis, plus de passable Advocats que Prescheurs, au moins en France." (I 10 39 B) A similar problem is posed by the obscure language of wills:

> Pourquoy est-ce que nostre langage commun, si aisé à tout autre usage, devient obscur et non intelligible en contract et testament, et que celuy qui s'exprime si clairement, quoy qu'il die et escrive, ne trouve en cela aucune maniere de se declarer qui ne tombe en doubte et contradiction? Si ce n'est que les princes de cet art, s'appliquans d'une peculiere attention à trier des mots solemnes et former des clauses artistes, ont tant poisé chaque sillabe, espluché si primement chaque espece de cousture, que les voilà enfrasquez et embrouillez en l'infinité des figures et si menuës partitions, qu'elles ne peuvent plus tomber soubs aucun reiglement et prescription ny aucune certaine intelligence. (III 13 1066-1067 B)

Montaigne's consideration of lawyers is closely connected with his commentary on judges and judicial language and on the law in general. He subsequently pursues this argument at length and alludes to political disputes, the outcome of which apparently favors those most adept in currying favor.

In addition to the language of medicine and law, Montaigne criticizes and removes the mask from that of predication and divination (II 12 585-586 A), attacks grandiloquence and oratorical language (I 10 39 A), and impugns literary sophistry and quibbling in principle, but allows that they may exercise a positive, utilitarian effect: "Ce sont voirement subtilitez, par où elle nous esveille souvent bien vainement. Les autheurs, mesmes plus serrez et plus sages, voiez autour d'un bon argument combien ils en sement d'autres legers et, qui y regarde de pres, incorporels. Ce ne sont qu'arguties verbales, qui nous trompent. Mais d'autant que ce peut estre utilement, je ne les veux pas autrement esplucher." (III 12 1039-1040 C) Theoretical language is more emphatically condemned elsewhere, as in the following passage: "(A) Un Rhetoricien du temps passé disoit que son mestier estoit, de choses petites les faire paroistre et trouver grandes. (B) C'est un cordonnier qui sait faire de grands souliers à un petit pied. (A) On luy eut faict donner le fouet en Sparte, de faire profession d'un' art piperesse et mensongere." (I 51 305) Finally, a more pointed and terse comment resumes Montaigne's fundamental attitude toward rhetoric: "Fy de l'eloquence qui nous laisse envie de soy, non des choses...." (I 40 252 A)

Montaigne also alludes to poets whose subject eludes them (I 17 72 A) and mentions philosophical language, subject to misinterpretation according to one's own predispositions: "Voyez demener et agiter Platon. Chacun, s'honorant de l'appliquer à soi, le couche du coté qu'il le veut. (II, 12, 587 C) Then there are the courtiers whose speech is so limited as to render them unfit to speak of anything other than the court: "Ce que je dis de ceux là me ramentoit, en chose semblable, ce que j'ay par fois aperçeu en aucuns de noz jeunes courtisans. Ils ne tiennent qu'aux hommes de leur sorte, nous regardent comme gens de l'autre monde, avec desdain ou pitié. Ostez leur les entretiens des mysteres de la court, ils sont hors de leur gibier, aussi neufs pour nous et malhabiles comme nous sommes à eux. On dict bien vray qu'un honneste homme c'est un homme meslé." (III 9 986 B) Montaigne speaks sympathetically of leaders who, striking counterfeit coin, lie to their subjects. (II 16 629 A)

In general terms Montaigne's comments concerning occupationally specific language deal directly with its effect on language in general and on the misunderstanding and confusion it engenders. Montaigne combats these abuses by exposing and mocking them. And finally, Montaigne affirms the philosophical limitations of speech: "Nostre parler a ses foiblesses et ses defauts, comme tout le reste. La plus part des occasions des troubles du monde sont Grammairiennes. Nos procez ne naissent que du debat de l'interpretation des loix; et la plus part des guerres, de cette impuissance de n'avoir sçeu clairement exprimer les conventions et traictez d'accord des princes. Combien de querelles et combien importantes a produit au monde le doubte du sens de cette syllabe, HOC!" (II 12 527 A)

The Ambiguity of Language

As Montaigne's comments on language and life and on the types of language employed by members of various professions give us to understand, he is profoundly aware that he lives "...in a world as theater, where public role and private self may diverge, a world where language does not communicate truth unequivocally but allows ambiguity and shifting meaning."[60] For Montaigne, "It is less that language is inherently misleading than that it is neutral; since there is no absolute relationship between words as symbols and that which they signify, they are operable on either side of truth."[61] And, in fact, there is a great deal of ambiguity in language, for words can mean much more than they say.[62] Language is inadequate to depict the whole truth or meaning. Truth may lie in the appropriate.

Although the ambiguity of language and Montaigne's concern with it is an underlying theme throughout the *Essais*, he treats it in greatest detail in the "Apologie." Here, as we have stated above, Montaigne speaks of the ambiguity and misinterpretation to which language is open, particularly in a philosophical and religious sense, and he states that a great deal of philosophical confusion results from the ambiguity of language. Furthermore, he believes that people are aware of the equivocal nature of language and that some deliberately misappropriate language and hide behind a cloud of difficult and unintelligible meanings: "Il s'est caché soubs le nuage de paroles et sens difficiles et non intelligibles...." (II 12 552 A) Montaigne continues with a discussion of decisive words and, citing the Bible and soothsayers as examples, speaks of their interpretation. Words can be used in many ways and understood in as many, especially when language is not specific but vague. He also states that different people call the same thing by different names. Such a divergence compounds the confusion brought about by indefinite language. Montaigne evokes this theme in conjunction with topics treated above. For example, he discusses the ambiguous and obscure language of pedants (I 25 136 C), as partially cited above, and the veiled terminology of contracts and wills (III 13 1066 B). Likewise Montaigne adduces numerous explanations assigned to literature and history; it is his belief that they obscure rather than clarify the meaning of the phenomena:

> Je ne sçay qu'en dire, mais il se sent par experience que tant d'interpretations dissipent la verité et la rompent. Aristote a escrit pour estre entendu; s'il ne l'a peu, moins le fera un moins habile et un tiers que celuy qui traite sa propre imagination. Nous ouvrons la matiere et l'espandons en la destrempant; d'un subject nous en faisons mille, et retombons, en multipliant et subdivisant, à l'infinité des atomes d'Epicurus. Jamais deux hommes ne jugerent pareillement de mesme chose, et est impossible de voir deux opinions semblables exactement, non seulement en divers hommes, mais en mesme homme à diverses heures. Ordinairement je trouve à doubter en ce que le commentaire n'a daigné toucher. Je bronche plus volontiers en pays plat, comme certains chevaux que je connois, qui chopent plus souvent en chemin uny. (III 13 1067 B)

Thus, for Montaigne, the mind is perpetually in quest of meaning and intelligibility, but yet discovers much ambiguity and little certainty. The world is a shifting, ever-changing place; and language, which should serve to further understanding among men, is often employed to perplex rather than to make plain. Whether or not their speaker or writer intends to deceive, the words themselves take on new dimensions by virtue of their various connotations. Montaigne sees language as a reflection of the world—continuously escaping our grasp, despite our efforts to capture it, no matter how well-intentioned we may be.

Does the intellectual plane of language fail to serve as a philosophical justification for man? If one believes that truth is not discernible—that illusion and reality are hopelessly confused—this would be so, certainly. What is "philosophical justification?" Proof man has *value?* Or indication he has an ethical nature? The intellectual does appear to justify man philosophically. It is no religious or ideal justification. It *is* basically rational. The intellect defines truth and *can* ascertain it as a continuing thing; but this does not negate the search—we can approach it, know what it is in a particular place, moment, or time, knowing it may be different tomorrow. This is why reliance upon the doctrinaire is dangerous and misleading.

In Montaigne's *epoch* ignorance is a sin—is self-destructive. One must *continue* to know, continue to define *reality*, be able to know it, hidden or revealed. And this is possible if one is intellectually alive to change and dialectically aware. On a philosophical level, innocence is less rational. The increase of sophistication brings more distance from the world. The more objective one is, the more removed one is. Therefore, there is a greater possibility for the misuse of an instrument which attempts to rejoin two things so far separated from one another.

As we see Montaigne's world view emerging on a philosophical and intellectual level through the medium of language, we begin to understand that his excursion through the world of ideas is fraught with pitfalls. For, who may presume to define and differentiate reality and illusion? Man can only try to render reality in words with all the sincerity he can muster, but Montaigne does not bury his head in the sand—he knows that there will always be men who will deliberately exploit the shifting nature of the world to their own advantage and others' detriment. When Montaigne satirizes professional jargon, when he speaks of mask, of ambiguity, of pedagogy, he is indirectly referring to liars and the seams they unravel in the social fabric, an ethical consideration, to be discussed at length in the second chapter.

The Inadequacy of Language: Depicting the Inscrutable

Faith

Montaigne feels that language is incapable of truly comprehending faith. His position may be explained as follows: "Vient ensuite, dans l'esprit du fidéisme, la dépossession de la raison, puis la critique du langage, la négation d'une position privilégiée de l'homme par rapport à l'animal, la réduction du concept de beauté à sa relativité ethnographique, et tout de suite après, à propos du passage des *Métamorphoses* d'Ovide que nous avons cité, cette remarque sarcastique à l'adresse du symbolisme anatomique que le chameau et l'autruche tendent beaucoup mieux que l'homme la tête vers le ciel,—qu'a donc l'homme à être si prétentieux?"[63]

In many cases language is used to obscure the truth, but Montaigne is aware that faith alone can aid us in making the leap from human to divine reason. Men tend to arrive at elaborate proofs for the existence of God, yet Montaigne refuses to accept these proofs, preferring to rely on faith rather than reason when the concept of the divine is involved. God must be classified among the rationally unknowable. Montaigne often mentions God, but always with the consciousness that he can never know whether he is right or wrong about the extent to which He is knowable. Montaigne can impart his own ideas; notwithstanding, even as he does so, he calls to our attention his own hesitation: "Je propose les fantasies humaines et miennes, simplement comme humaines fantasies, et separement considerées, non comme arrestés et reglées par l'ordonnance celeste, incapables de doubte et d'altercation: matiere d'opinion, non matiere de foy; ce que je discours selon moy, non ce que je croy selon Dieu, comme les enfans proposent leurs essais: intruisable[*sic*], non instruisants; d'une maniere laïque, non clericale, mais tres-religieuse tousjours. (I 56 323 C)

Furthermore, he feels this is as it should be, and he cites as an example a chronicle of the South American Indians and their prophets who are put to death if their presage prove wrong. As they engage in divination, they usurp God's wisdom; therefore, they richly deserve their fate: "C'est don de Dieu que la divination: voylà pourquoy ce devroit estre une imposture punissable, d'en abuser." (I 31 208 C) This brood—seers, soothsayers, sybils, etc.—enthrall the language to serve their own ends, for they can not possibly know what they profess to know: "Le vray champ et subject de l'imposture sont les choses inconnuës. D'autant qu'en premier lieu l'estrangeté mesme donne credit; et puis, n'estant point subjectes à nos discours ordinaires, elles nous ostent le moyen de les combattre." (I 32 215 A)

In addition, Montaigne believes that religion often becomes for men a game of meaningless words, and he sees man as essentially incapable of understanding and interpreting the words of God. As for attempts to interpret the Bible, Montaigne believes that men simply quarrel over terminology without truly understanding the import of a message. As Friedrich puts it: "...quand on autorise l'individu à trancher lui-même en matière de religion, l'infirmité essentielle de l'homme, sa prétention à atteindre la certitude par le raisonnement, devient une maladie aiguë, dégénère en querelle de mots...."[64]

Certainly, Montaigne critics comment on his attitudes toward the inscrutables in our lives, and much of the material examined concentrates on the difficulty of spanning the chasm between man and God. In essence, as Thibaudet points out: "C'est que nos disputes sont grammairiennes, qu'elle proviennent de nostre discours, et notre discours se meut dans l'être, il donne l'être à tout ce dont il parle, il exprime tout comme réalité et affirmation...Si nous ne pouvons concevoir le néant, c'est que l'être du langage, notre être, nous suit partout. Si nous ne pouvons concevoir le désordre, c'est que notre langage, notre être, que nous portons avec nous, constitue un ordre."[65] Doubtless this is true of Montaigne's attitude toward language. He always retains the semblance of the Pyhrronic python. He disbelieves the assumption that there exists a means whereby man can know truth absolutely or whereby man can grasp truth with words.[66] And, although Montaigne sometimes attempts to verbalize his thought concerning God, more often he relegates God to the realm of the unknowable, an enigma that man can never resolve through reason. It is a fact of man's existence that the unknown and the unknowable exist, and Montaigne, no dupe, does not contest this fact. He contents himself with what he knows. For the rest, he yields to faith or to the realm of unanswerable questions. Although Montaigne is criticized for not incorporating more Christian elements in his work, notably by Auerbach: "Er hätte die christlichen Zeugnisse für seine Anschauung noch bedeutend vermehren können; er hätte vor allem die Fleischwerdung des Wortes selbst zu Hilfe rufen können,"[67] it appears that Montaigne's whole Weltanschauung is fundamentally Christian. He may not be greatly interested in metaphysics, but he is concerned with man living morally and ethically in the world. He may be Catholic by reason of Catholicism's humanistic implications, as Thibaudet claims,[68] but this theory seems irrelevant to the main point—that is, that Montaigne is more concerned with the present than the hereafter, and this is as true of his attitude toward faith as it is of his attitude toward life, love, death, or any other pivotal topic.

Death

Death is, of course, one of the most difficult aspects of life to confront men, and language often reflects attempts to allay or avoid this ultimate fact of the human condition: "Parce que cette syllabe frappoit trop rudement leurs oreilles, et que cette voix leur sembloit malencontreuse, les Romains avoyent appris de l'amollir ou de l'estendre en perifrazes. Au lieu de dire: il est mort; il a cessé de vivre, disent-ils, il a vescu. Pourveu que ce soit vie, soit elle passée, il[*sic*] se consolent. Nous en avons emprunté nostre feu Maistre-Jehan." (I 20 84 B) In addition, Montaigne speaks of his own contemplation of death: "...aussi ay-je pris en coustume d'avoir, non seulement en l'imagination, mais continuellement la mort en la bouche; et n'est rien dequoy je m'informe si volontiers, que de la mort des hommes: quelle parole, quel visage, quelle contenance ils y ont eu; ny endroit des histoires, que je remarque si attantifvement," (I 20 90 A) and of his attitude toward his own death and human rituals concerning dying: "Je me contente d'une mort recueillie en soy, quiete et solitaire, toute mienne, convenable à ma vie retirée et privée. Au rebours de la superstition Romaine, où l'on estimoit malheureux celuy qui mouroit sans parler et qui n'avoit ses plus proches à luy clorre les yeux, j'ay assez affaire à me consoler sans avoir à consoler autruy, assez de pensées en la teste sans que les circonstances m'en apportent de nouvelles, et assez de matiere à m'entretenir sans l'emprunter." (III 9 979 B) Furthermore, he believes that most people are born, live, and die without being remembered after their death: "Dix mille bons compaignons et plusieurs grands capitaines moururent à sa suite, vaillamment et courageusement, desquels les noms n'ont duré qu'autant que leurs femmes et leurs enfants vesquirent...." (II 16 628 A)

Montaigne often mentions the direct link between language and death. At times it is language which directly occasions death. For example, he tells the story of a woman who, as a result of the incontinence of her speech, commits suicide:

> Il ne se peut rien adjouster à la delicatesse de la mort de la femme de Fulvius, familier d'Auguste. Auguste, ayant descouvert qu'il avoit esventé un secret important qu'il luy avoit fié, un matin qu'il le vint voir, luy en fit une maigre mine. Il s'en retourna au logis, plain de desespoir; et dict tout piteusement à sa femme qu'estant tombé en ce malheur il estoit resolu de se tuer. Elle tout franchement: Tu ne feras que raison, veu qu'ayant assez souvent experimenté l'incontinance de ma langue, tu ne t'en es point donné de garde. Mais laisse, que je me tue la premiere. Et, sans autrement marchander, se donna d'une espée dans le corps. (II 3 358 B)

In this instance, Montaigne simply recounts the story; he makes no comment on it. At other times, language becomes part of the process of dying. For instance, he tells of the lingering death of prisoners about whom he can think of nothing worse than their not being able to express themselves:

> Je n'imagine aucun estat pour moy si insupportable et horrible, que d'avoir l'ame vifve et affligée, sans moyen de se declarer: comme je dirois de ceux qu'on envoye au supplice, leur ayant couppé la langue, si ce n'estoit qu'en cette sorte de mort la plus muette me semble la mieux seante, si elle est accompaignée d'un ferme visage et grave; et comme ces miserables prisonniers qui tombent és mains des vilains bourreaux soldats de ce temps, desquels ils sont tourmentez de toute espece de cruel traictement pour les contraindre à quelque rançon excessive et impossible, tenus cependant en condition et en lieu où ils n'ont moyen quelconque d'expression et signification de leurs pensées et de leur misere. (II 51 375 B)

Montaigne also speaks of the Roman gladiators who face death courageously: "C'estoit, à la verité, un merveilleux exemple, et de tres-grand fruict pour l'institution du peuple, de voir tous les jours en sa presence cent, deux cens, et mille couples d'hommes, armez les uns contre les autres, se hacher en pieces avecques une si extreme fermeté de courage qu'on ne leur vist lâcher une parolle de foiblesse ou commiseration, jamais tourner le dos, ny faire seulement un mouvement lâche pour gauchir au coup de leur adversaire, ains tendre le col à son espée et se presenter au coup." (II 23 684 A) He professes also to admire a king who shows great courage in the face of death "Le Roy, plantant fierement et rigoreusement les yeux sur luy, pour reproche de sa lascheté et pusillanimité, luy dict seulement ces mots, d'une voix rude et ferme: Et moy, suis-je dans un bain? suis-je pas plus à mon aise que toy?...Ils le pendirent depuis, ayant courageusement entrepris de se delivrer par armes d'une si longue captivité et subjection, où il fait sa fin digne d'un magnamine prince." (III 6 912 B)

In addition, language can also give us a clue to the workings of the subconscious mind, and it can warn us of the danger of approaching death from suicide. Once again he tells a story to illustrate this point. It deals with a woman who speaks with words and gestures which give her listeners a clue to the fact that she is considering suicide: "Ces paroles, avec plusieurs autres signes, firent sentir à ses parents qu'elle estoit pour se deffaire elle-mesme, impatiente de supporter la fortune de son mary." (II 35 746 A)

Language is also connected with the mourning which follows death, and, as has been previously mentioned, this mourning is lamentably often counterfeit. For example, Montaigne censures the conquistadors for torturing the King of Mexico to death and for then having feigned mourning for him: "Et puis, pour endormir les peuples estonnez et transis de chose si estrange, on contrefit un grand deuil de sa mort, et luy ordonna l'on des somptueuses funerailles." (III 6 912 B)

Lastly he speaks of the connection between language and the dying. For many, it is contrary to their sense of duty to allow one to die in peace. Instead they suffocate him with words. What we need according to Montaigne is wise men to help us to depart life, men who will not make our final hours miserable with foolish conversation: "C'est contre le devoir et est tesmoignage de peu d'affection et de peu de soing de vous laisser mourir en repos: l'un tourmente vos yeux, l'autre vos oreilles, l'autre la bouche; il n'y a sens ny membre qu'on ne vous fracasse. Le coeur vous serre de pitié d'ouyr les plaintes des amis, et de despit à l'avanture d'ouyr d'autres plaintes feintes et masquées." (III 9 978 B)

Parslow, in examining Montaigne's attitude toward death, feels Montaigne believes that "...death is a natural part of life, and Nature herself must have provided us with the necessary resources for meeting it. The evidence for this is that simple people and animals die with as much or more composure than philosophers. Therefore, the natural and best way to prepare for death is not to think about it but to rely on Nature to show us the way when the time comes."[69]

It is difficult enough to remove the masks from human intention, to obtain contingent human truth, but the difficulty man faces when he encounters the inscrutable appears insurmountable. There is only the certainty of pain and love and death. These touch us but their meaning, their cause, the metaphorical intention behind them, whether or not they are masks, are questions about which the application of the intellectual can give no assurance and to which the application of language is less successful or meaningful. The fact of death is with us; words do nothing to mitigate it. The supernatural may exist, but words as instruments of reason can tell us nothing of it, only more about ourselves. Here reliance must be on nature not on words, which appear only foolish in the encounter with the unreasonable. The mind may be separate from the world; but the gap may be bridged. The gap to the unreasonable is, however, totally unbridgeable by reason.

Words can describe the approach of death, our encounter with its approach, our reason confronting it, but there is no direct link by word to death, except of the most tangential sort. The gulf between man and God can be crossed only by faith.

The relation of speech to death and pain is to be as carefully considered as the relation of speech to any of the concerns of daily living. It too has an ethical—that is, appropriate aspect. Language which is manipulated into illusion and mask in the political and practical spheres for particular individual advantage is also conducive to manipulation in the area of the inscrutable. Its aspect here may be less culpable morally, but a façade to obscure the real is nevertheless apparent, and it so constitutes an insincere action which can serve, Montaigne avers, no good purpose. Euphemism has no effect upon the reality of death. Words may attempt its mitigation but to no avail. Any attempt to fool oneself only diminishes the self. The implication is that the reality of intention (God's?) obscured is evil. Montaigne's view is that any attempt at obscurantism in terms of such an inscrutable as death can be little other than presumption on man's part. God's truth is not to be so prescribed.

In essence, the import of Montaigne's thinking on death seems to be that one should concentrate on living well—dying well will follow by itself. Throughout Montaigne's work, life is regarded as more important than death. He sees it as a subject to be treated like any other and nothing so extraordinary as to be sacrosanct. In fact, as Nolan pointed out: "Montaigne did not hesitate to add a touch of the comic to his serious discussions of death."[70]

Pain

Closely linked to Montaigne's utterances on death are his comments on pain, and, in fact, he makes a comparison between pain and words and pain and death: "(A) Bien, me dira lon, vostre regle serve à la mort, mais que direz vous de l'indigence? Que direz vous encor de la douleur, que (C) Aristippus,

Hieronymus et (A) la plupart des sages ont estimé le dernier mal; et ceux qui le nioient de parole, le confessoient par effet?" (I 14 55) He also speaks of the reverse syndrome—that is, the effect of pain on words or on speech: "Je me taste au plus espais du mal et ay tousjours trouvé que j'estoy capable de dire, de penser, de respondre aussi sainement qu'en une autre heure; mais non si constamment, la douleur me troublant et destournant. Quant on me tient le plus atterré et que les assistants m'espargnent, j'essaye souvent mes forces et entame moy-mesmes des propos les plus esloignez de mon estat. Je puis tout par un soudain effort; mais ostez en la durée." (II 37 762 C)

By and large, Montaigne seems to feel that people invent euphemisms for pain as well as death because they can not bear to brave the reality of their evil: "Les noms mesme de quoy ils appellent les maladies en adoucissent et amollissent l'aspreté: la phtisie c'est la tous pour eux; la dysenterie, devoyement d'estomac; un pleuresis, c'est un morfondement; et selon qu'ils les nomment doucement, ils les supportent aussi." (III 12 104 B) He also sees that words are used as medicine to alleviate pain: "On te voit suer d'ahan, pallir, rougir, trembler, vomir jusques au sang, souffrir des contractions et convulsions estranges, degouter par foys de grosses larmes des yeux, rendre les urines espesses, noires, et effroyables, ou les avoir arrestées par quelque pierre espineuse et herissé qui te pouinct et escorche cruellement le col de la verge, entretenant cependant les assistans d'une contenance commune, bouffonnant à pauses avec tes gens, tenant ta partie en un discours tendu, excusant de parolle ta douleur et rabatant de ta souffrance." (III 13 1091 B) They are in this instance more powerful than the most potent remedies of the time. Apparently, to summarize his discussion of pain, we might cite this declaration: "Enfant, tu és venu au monde pour endurer; endure, souffre, et tais toy." (III 13 1089 B) Finally, Frame quotes one of Montaigne's later additions as follows: "To reject pain is to reject life and man's estate."[71]

Love

In addition to pain and death and man's attempt to relate them in language, Montaigne deals with love and the attempt to capture and enhance this ephemeral passion with words: "Combien de jeux tres lascivement plaisants naissent de l'honneste et vergongneuse manière de parler des ouvrages de l'amour! (II 15 613 C) At the same time, he emphasizes the difficulty of rendering this emotion in words and the importance of gesture in communicating tender sentiments: "... une oeillade, une inclination, une parolle, un signe." (III 5 880 B)

From his treatment of love, let us move to the topic of women and language: "Il faut croire que le coeur leur fremit d'effroy, que le son de nos mots blesse la pureté de leurs oreilles, qu'elles nous en haissent et s'accordent à nostre importunité d'une force forcée." (II 15 615 A) In general, Montaigne appears to regard women as apt to be easily misled by words.

So does he recommend that when consoling an aggrieved woman, we must adopt a certain kind of language and manner and that we must use words to divert her attention to more pleasant subjects. (III 4 830-831 B) To Montaigne's mind, women are not properly reared: "Nous les dressons des l'enfance aus entremises de l'amour: leur grace, leur atiffeure, leur science, leur parole, toute leur instruction ne regarde qu' à ce but. Leurs gouvernantes ne leur impriment autre chose que le visage de l'amour, ne fut qu'en le leur representant continuellement pour les en desgouster." (III 5 856 B) He also feels they are often childish or impudent: "Je suis fort serviteur de la nayfveté et de la liberté; mais il n'y a remede: si elle n'est du tout niaise ou enfantine, elle est inepte aus dames, et messeante en ce commerce; elle gauchit incontinent sur l'impudence." (III 5 867 B) He envisions women as devious, yet submissive, creatures when, for example, he writes: "J'ay veu aussi, pour cet effect de divertir les opinions et conjectures du peuple et desvoyer les parleurs, des femmes couvrir leurs vrayes affections par des affections contrefaictes. Mais j'en ay veu telle qui, en se contrefaisant, s'est laissée prendre à bon escient, et a quitté la vraye et originelle affection pour la feinte; et aprins par elle que ceux qui se trouvent bien logez sont des sots de consentir à ce masque." (III 4 836 B) In this case, language affects life and alters reality.

The Unconscious

Montaigne's treatment of the unconscious is limited. He mentions it as a real fact: "Il nous advient ainsi sur le beguayement du sommeil, avant qu'il nous ait du tout saisis, de sentir comme en songe ce qui se faict autour de nous, et suyvre les voix d'une ouye trouble et incertaine qui semble ne donner qu'aux bords de l'ame; et faisons des responses, à la suitte des dernieres paroles qu'on nous a dites, qui ont plus de fortune que de sens." (II 6 375 A) But here again he does not attempt to categorize or to ascertain truth concerning the unconscious mind. With regard to a pre-Freudian era, it is sufficient to note that he appears to foreknow its existence and that he believes that it is connected with language in some basic ways.

Summary Comment

We have seen Montaigne, intellectual, imprisoned in the universe but attempting to bring order to a disorderly world in order to deal with it on a practical level, finding the application of language and reason inadequate to the search for and depiction of those inscrutable aspects of our lives. In general, then, he treats such topics gingerly because they constitute a stumbling block upon which language falters. As he says of prayer, he might consider such indefinables better verbalized by the conscience than by the tongue.

This is not to mean, though, that the search for truth is to be abandoned, but rather that for those of a skeptical mind the possibility of achieving certitude in these areas is not possible. As we have seen, however, a less circumscribed certitude might be achieved in the search for knowledge of man's individual nature; for language—carefully applied—is able to depict with some accuracy both his inner self and that world exterior to him. It is that which is most receptive to the application of reason which most interests Montaigne. As Frame points out: "Montaigne's central concern was always man and his life, why we behave as we do...his interest is in the here and now, not in the unknowable...."[72] He seeks knowledge applicable to life, useful to the construction of a coherent social order. One's duty is to describe, then, what can be described as honestly as one is able with language which most accurately will reflect the thing or the idea. It is such an appropriate use of language which is essential both to the search for knowledge about the self and others and to its further and profitable application to the essential problems of living; for, as we shall see, for Montaigne—the use one makes of language becomes a moral issue.

CHAPTER II

The Language Of Ethical Action: The Expression Of Truth

Language and Virtue: The Willful Expression of Truth

The Self-Portrait: A Commitment of Integrity

In the first chapter we have dealt with Montaigne, the thinker, attempting through the judicious use of language to arrive at general principles and a philosophy of life. In the second chapter we move to a consideration of Montaigne, the man, living in the world and attempting to arrive at ethical solutions to the abstract problems suggested in Chapter I. Here we see Montaigne as a particular person, totally human, pursuing his affairs in the world, developing moral and ethical principles for himself and mankind in general and revealing the crucial role of language in that development.

As a man portraying himself in action in the world, Montaigne claims to wish to portray himself completely and truthfully, and he utters many statements bearing upon the sincerity of his attempt to portray himself through language. He goes so far in his portrait as to admit that he lied about how much money he had, certainly a very human foible. He mocks himself for being so petty: "J'en faisoy un secret: et moy, qui ose tant dire de moy, ne parloy de mon argent qu'en mensonge, comme font les autres, qui s'appauvrissent riches, s'enrichissent pauvres, et dispensent leur conscience de jamais tesmoigner sincerement de ce qu'ils ont: Ridicule et honteuse prudence." (I 14 64 C) On the other hand, he contrasts this somewhat trifling prevarication with the manner in which man must face death: "Mais à ce dernier rolle de la mort et de nous, il n'y a plus que faindre, il faut parler François, il faut montrer ce qu'il y a de bon et de net dans le fond du pot,

Nam verae voces tum demum pectore ab imo
Ejiciuntur, et eripitur persona, manet res." (I 19 80 A)

However, he claims to make no doctrinaire moral pronouncements: "Je ne me mesle pas de dire ce qu'il faut faire au monde, d'autres assés s'en meslent, mais ce que j'y fay. *Mihi sic usus est; tibi, ut opus est facto, face.*" (I

28 192 C) Thus, he claims merely to portray himself. This self-portrait stresses his wish to converse with people of like background and experience so that they will be better able to grasp the truth of his statements: "Tout ainsi que cil qui fut rencontré à chevauchons sur un baton, se jouant avec ses enfants, pria l'homme qui l'y surprint, de n'en rien dire jusques à ce qu'il fut pere luy-mesme, estimant que la passion qui luy naistroit lors en l'ame le rendroit juge equitable d'une telle action: je souhaiterois aussi parler à des gens qui eussent essayé ce que je dis." (I 28 192 A)

Of himself, he says that he has never learned to be a flatterer: "...et ne m'entens pas en lettres ceremonieuses, qui n'ont autre substance que d'une belle enfileure de paroles courtoises. Je n'ay ny la faculté ny le goust de ces longues offres d'affection et de service. Je n'en crois pas tant, et me desplaist d'en dire guiere outre ce que j'en crois...Je hay à mort de sentir au flateur...." (I 40 252-253 B) Moreover, his aim in writing is not so much to establish the truth as to seek it. Fully aware that such a goal renders him vulnerable to criticism, particularly from the Church,

> (A) Je propose des fantasies informes et irresolues, comme font ceux qui publient des questions doubteuses, à debattre aux escoles: non pour establir la verité, mais pour la chercher. Et les soubmets au jugement de ceux à qui il touche de regler, non seulement mes actions et mes escris, mais encore mes pensées. Esgalement m'en sera acceptable et utile la condemnation comme l'approbation, (C) tenant pour execrable, s'il se trouve chose ditte par moy ignorament ou inadvertament contre les sainctes prescriptions de l'Eglise catholique, apostolique et Romaine, en laquelle je meurs et en laquelle je suis nay. (A) Et pourtant, me remettant tousjours à l'authorité de leur censure, qui peut tout sur moy, je me mesle ainsin temerairement à toute sorte de propos, comme icy. (I 56 317-318)

he nonetheless refuses to lie about or to himself, for he detests both kinds of lies. (III 1 704 B)

Nor does he wish unreservedly to be beholden to the conscience of anyone else: "Je ne veux estre tenu serviteur ny si affectionné ny si loyal, qu'on me treuve bon à trahir personne. Qui est infidelle à soy mesme, l'est excusablement à son maistre." (III 1 794 B)

Returning to the self-portrait, he remarks that people should be bold in speaking of what they do, for it is important not to hide one's vices from others: (B) "Au reste, je me suis ordonné d'oser dire tout ce que j'ose faire, et me desplais des pensées mesmes impubliables. La pire de mes actions et conditions ne me semble pas si laide comme je trouve laid et lâche de ne l'oser avouer. Chacun est discret en la confession, on le devoit estre en l'action: la hardiesse de faillir est aucunement compensée et bridée par la hardiesse de le confesser....Ceux qui le celent à autruy, le celent ordinairement à eux mesmes. " (III 5 845)

In effect, lying seems more odious to him than adultery. (III 5 846 B) As for himself, he never belies his word, and, although he calls himself stupidly conscientious, "Si elles ont voulu essayer la liberté de mon jugement, je ne me suis pas feint à leur donner des advis paternels et mordans, et à les pinser où il leur cuysoit. Si je leur ay laissé à se plaindre de moy, c'est plustost d'y avoir trouvé un amour, au pris de l'usage moderne, sottement consciencieux. J'ay observé ma parolle ès choses dequoy on m'eut ayséement dispensé; elles se rendoyent lors par fois avec reputation, et soubs des capitulations qu'elles souffroyent ayséement estre faucées par le vaincueur," (III 5 889-890 B) this qualification suggests covert self-satisfaction. In addition, he alludes to people in general and their reactions vis-à-vis someone who speaks of himself. He claims that if a person speaks badly of himself, he will be believed, but if he speaks well of himself, people will think him a liar: "Publiant et accusant mes imperfections, quelqu'un apprendra de les craindre. Les parties que j'estime le plus en moy, tirent plus d'honneur de m'accuser que de me recommander. Voilà pourquoi j'y retombe et m'y arreste plus souvant. Mais, quand tout est conté, on ne parle jamais de soy sans perte. Les propres condemnations sont tousjours accruës, les louanges mescruës." (III 8 922 B)

Continuing with the self-portrait, Montaigne claims to utter words intended not to relieve his misfortune or suffering, but rather to steel his courage to bear them with fortitude: "Ce m'est faveur que la desolation de mon aage: je souffre plus volontiers que mes maux en soient rechargez, que si mes biens en eussent esté troublez. Les paroles que j'exprime au malheur sont paroles de despit; mon courage se herisse au lieu de s'applatir." (III 9 947 B) With regard to his fellows, he chooses not to forego his basic sincerity lest he become a sycophant. As a matter of fact, he always speaks better of his friends after their deaths: "Ceux qui ont merité de moy de l'amitié et de la reconnoissance ne l'ont jamais perdue pour n'y estre plus: je les ay mieux payez et plus soigneusement, absens et ignorans. Je parle plus affectueusement de mes amis quand il n'y a plus moyen qu'ils le sçachent." (III 9 996 B) Consequently, the self-portrait discloses an individual who attaches great importance to the moral virtues of sincerity and truth, one who does not want to break his word because he considers it all-important. When he says something, he feels he is promising it; therefore, he seldom speaks of his ideas: (B) J'aymeroy bien plus cher rompre la prison d'un muraille et des loix que de ma parole. (C) Je suis delicat à l'observation de mes promesses jusques à la superstition, et les fay en tous subjects volantiers incertaines et conditionnelles. A celles qui sont de nul poids je donne poids de la jalousie de ma regle: elle me gehenne et charge de son propre interest. Ouy, es entreprinses toutes miennes et libres, si j'en dy le poinct, il me semble que je me le prescry, et que le donner à la science d'autruy c'est le preordonner à soy...." (III 9 966-967)

As an individual who holds that it is essential to tell the truth about himself, he feels himself to be living in an era when such moral idealism seems anachronistic: "Mes moeurs mesmes, qui ne disconviennent de celles qui courent à peine de la largeur d'un poulce, me rendent pourtant aucunement farouche à mon aage, et inassociable. Je ne sçay pas si je me trouve desgouté sans raison du monde que je hante, mais je sçay bien que ce seroit sans raison si je me plaignois qu'il fut desgouté de moy plus que je le suis de luy." (III 9 991 C)

In discussing his term of office as mayor of Bordeaux, he claims that he deciphers himself to the citizenry as clearly and truthfully as he can: "A mon arrivée, je me deschiffray fidelement et conscientieusement, tout tel que je me sens estre: sans memoire, sans vigilance, sans experience, et sans vigueur; sans hayne aussi, sans ambition, sans avarice, et sans violence; à ce qu'ils fussent informez et instruicts de ce qu'ils avoyent à attendre de mon service." (III 10 1005 B) Criticizing public servants' interestedness in general, he thereby implies a contrast favorable to himself: "J'ay facilement oublié ceux que l'ambition mesle au devoir et couvre de son titre. Ce sont ceux qui le plus souvant remplissent les yeux et les oreilles, et contentent les hommes. Non pas la chose, mais l'apparence les paye. S'ils n'oyent du bruict, il leur semble qu'on dorme." (III 10 1021 B)

Although he is willing to act on several levels, he finds it necessary to have the time to retreat into himself:

> (B) Mes humeurs sont contradictoires aux humeurs bruyantes. J'arresterois bien un trouble sans me troubler, et chastierois un desordre sans alteration. Ay-je besoing de cholere et d'inflammation? Je l'emprunte et m'en masque. Mes meurs sont mousses, plutost fades qu'aspres. Je n'accuse pas un magistrat qui dorme, pourveu que ceux qui sont soubs sa main dorment quand et luy; les loix dorment de mesme. Pour moy, je louë une vie glissante, sombre et muette, (C) '*neque submissam et abjectam, neque se efferentem.*' (B) Ma fortune le veut ainsi. Je suis nay d'une famille qui a coulé sans esclat et sans tumulte, et de longue memoire particulierement ambitieuse de preud'hommie. (III 10 1021)

To Montaigne's mind, such an exaction derives from the contrast he evolves between the inward and outward reality of man, and it further illustrates the difference between himself and his contemporaries. Furthermore, he states that although he would like to retire from the world, he paradoxically finds himself continually attracted toward it: "Je me presche il y a si long temps de me tenir à moy, et separer des choses estrangeres; toutesfois je tourne encores tousjours les yeux à costé: l'inclination, un mot favorable d'un grand, un bon visage me tente. Dieu sçait s'il en est cherté en ce temps, et quel sens il porte!" (III 12 1045 B)

What is the contrast Montaigne evolves between the inward and outward realities of man? Are there two realities?

The inward reality involves a dialogue with the self. It is the reality of the individual human mind moving within its own memories and stored perceptions. His outward reality is the mind perceiving the world, the mind interacting with it. It is more involved with body and nature, with the world of man and individual responsibility.

The retreat from the world of which he speaks is a necessary and refreshing removal—a time of reflection and ideas, but its continuance into the indefinite is unsatisfactory for the rational man. The resources of the mind are limited, and his epistemological conclusions lead to continual interaction with the world—the only avenue to truth. The attraction of retreat is as paradoxical as the attraction of the world. Either can be fatal—one can lead to unreason (not innocence) and vulnerability, the other to the madness of the unendingly non-reflective, the obsessive "now," the unethical "self." There is, however, the attraction both present. And the attraction to "retreat" may mistakenly be equated with the attraction to the inscrutable otherness of the mystery of God. This *is* mistaken, for there is no escape from the living mind. Its extremity is not God but rather madness, which is something other than faith or ethical behavior, the latter of which requires involvement with the world.

The implications of Montaigne's thought are that there are certainly two realities if not more. Philosophically, there is the reality of God, his inscrutable impingement upon the second reality, the world of nature and men. Intellectually, there is the reality of the mind, its objectifying capacity and its resources in the material reality, the second reality of the intellect. That material reality itself presents to the reason the two realities in human terms of appearance and intention, which may involve game, or humor, or ethics.

However, Montaigne believes his redemption to lie in his characteristically bold and unconstrained speech. In effect, he states that he once owed his deliverance to the openness and firmness of his countenance: "Le plus apparent, qui se demasqua et me fit cognoistre son nom, me redict lors plusieurs fois que je devoy cette delivrance à mon visage, liberté et fermeté de mes parolles, qui me rendoyent indigne d'une telle mes-adventure, et me demanda asseurance d'une pareille." (III 12 1062 B) And finally, the indispensable role of memory in achieving truthfulness is acknowledged: "Et n'estoit que ce que je fay par faute de memoire, les autres le font encore plus souvant par faute de foy, je prendrois tousjours en chose de faict la verité de la bouche d'un autre plustost que de la mienne." (III 13 1074 B)

As was apparent in our treatment of the mask in the first chapter, there is extensive critical controversy concerning this theme and its application to Montaigne and the self-portrait. Many of Montaigne's affirmations are open to question, but in each instance he makes us aware of the mien behind the mask. The exaggerations and examples of false modesty serve to humanize the portrait which Montaigne paints in words rather than oils. In point of fact, Montaigne "...est capable de distinguer la vérité nue telle qu'elle apparaît à sa conscience et la vérité extérieure telle qu'elle s'organise en hyperbole et en corps enflé dans le bruit de la parole...."[73]

On the other hand, there are many touches in the self-portrait with which he deliberately exaggerates some aspects of himself. Frame for example recounts Montaigne's claims that his castle was the birthplace of his ancestors and that they gave the castle their name. In truth, the family adopted the name of the castle, and his father alone among his forebears was born there.[74] Also Montaigne was prone to exaggerate his military service, and he spent less time than he claimed in his tower library.[75]

In addition, Frame points out that, as is often the case when one indulges in self-deprecation, others are likely to believe the self-deprecation to be true. He states: "He was a man of more dedication than he claims and than he is often thought to have had."[76]

Despite such fibs, Frame believes that "...many sides of Montaigne change little if at all. His temper is always skeptical; he looks before any mental leap. His perspective shows him that the convictions of his time, his region, and himself may be anything but absolute truths."[77] In essence, Frame sees Montaigne as a man who is totally aware of the diversity of his time; as a consequence, he "...mistrusts...oversimplification...."[78] Frame further states that "...the change he finds everywhere, without and within, makes him wonder whether men ever harbor perfect truth or know it if they do."[79]

In general terms, many of the contradictions apparent in Montaigne's self-portrait are the result of his attempt to picture himself in the process of changing, of becoming. If there are small details in which he contradicts himself, if there are aspects of his background which he exaggerates, they nonetheless do not negate the composite image of a man attempting to portray himself and including in that portrait his vices as well as his virtues.

As Frame puts it: "For all of Montaigne's love of paradox and self-depreciation, his strong moral convictions are clear. A central commitment is to integrity. He refuses to break a promise even if extracted by fear."[80] In this event, when we consider Montaigne acting on a moral plane, "Integrity also implies truth."[81]

What is the fundamental role of language in creating the self-portrait and why does it result in contradictions? Is the nature of language such that they always occur?

There are various reasons one can cite which cause ambiguity and contradiction in the self-portrait itself. Since Montaigne has stated that one could best be understood by those of like background and experience, considerable contradiction might now appear in the *Essais*. Obviously he sought out compatriots because the ambiguity of words and their multiple associations would be so limited and his meaning readily understood. It is in the nature of language and time that contradictions will appear even in work which is written with attention to clarity and minimization of mask.

While it seems that mask is usually employed for unscrupulous and selfish ends—to obscure true intention, there are times when ambiguity and a kind of mask seem inherently virtuous. As we have observed, Montaigne feels understatement and self-deprecation civilized. It is the nature of mean-spirited men to boast. The gentleman might find himself affecting a mask less attractive than himself, less "serious" than himself, for he does not desire to be bothersome to others. The essential element of such a mask is the understanding one has with one's audience, with one's friend in conversation, in behavior, that the self will be known, nevertheless, but that some discipline, some element of selflessness has mitigated the unattractive. This is the element of manners and the sense of the appropriate.

True virtue lies in the coincidence of its inner reality and its outward appearance, but ironically the outward appearance of goodness is understood to be purposefully belied by one's words about oneself. Goodness may require mask.

The many problems of ambiguity of the appropriation of the uncivilized mask involving abuse of language are not relevant here in the self-portrait, of course. Or at least not intentionally so. Montaigne would be the last to say, however, that he knows his intentions absolutely. The *process* of truth in the self-portrait admits change. And it is in the nature of language to attempt a definition of a thing or concept in *time*.

Virtue: The Relationship of Conscience, Deed, and Language

Above all, Montaigne is a moralist; and he exists, perhaps most vividly, on the moral plane, for he appears to see himself most clearly in the practical realm of usual moral and ethical problems.

Consequently, one of Montaigne's central concerns is with virtue—its real or feigned presence or absence in persons and their deeds. Without qualm, he cites the Latin: "*Odi homines ignava opera, philosopha sententia.*" (I 25 135 A) In fact, he satirizes those who study Greek and Latin and the virtues propounded in classical culture without becoming more virtuous themselves:

> (A) Nous nous enquerons volontiers: Sçait-il du Grec ou du Latin? escrit-il en vers ou en prose? Mais s'il est devenu meilleur ou plus advisé, c'estoit le principal, et c'est ce qui

> demeure derriere. Il falloit s'enquerir qui est mieux sçavant, non qui est plus sçavant. Nous ne travaillons qu'à remplir la memoire, et laissons l'entendement (C) et la conscience (A) vuide. Tout ainsi que les oyseaux vont quelquefois à la queste du grein, et le portent au bec sans le taster, pour en faire bechée à leurs petits, ainsi nos pedantes vont pillotant la science dans les livres, et ne la logent qu'au bout de leurs lévres, pour la dégorger seulement et mettre au vent. (I 25 136)

He speaks pejoratively of the pedants who pretend to be very learned, but whose pretense alters nothing of their basic want of moral integrity; it alters only their outward appearance: "Mais, qui pis est, leurs escholiers et leurs petits ne s'en nourrissent et alimentent non plus; ains elle passe de main en main, pour cette seule fin d'en faire parade, d'en entretenir autruy, et d'en faire des contes, comme une vaine monnoye, inutile à tout autre usage et emploite qu'à compter et jetter. '*Apud alios loqui didicerunt, non ipsi secum.*" "*Non est loquendum, sed gubernandum.*" (I 25 136-137 A) In effect, he also holds that the reverse should be true.

He insists that the conscience and virtue of a person be reflected in his speech: "Qu'il ne luy demande pas seulement compte des mots de sa leçon, mais du sens et de la substance, et qu'il juge du profit qu'il aura fait, non par le tesmoignage de sa memoire, mais de sa vie," (I 26 151 A) and that language and morality be reflected in the individual's life: "Le vray miroir de nos discours est le cours de nos vies." (I 26 168 C)

Furthermore, Montaigne lists the virtues which he thinks most conducive to sound moral existence: "...diligence, pourvoyance, patience, discipline, subtilité, magnanimité, resolution, bonheur...." (II 36 754-755 A) He also speaks of good deeds and their relationship to good conscience and, ultimately concluding that virtue is its own reward and the only payment which never fails us, he enumerates some more attributes he deems qualities:

> Il n'est pareillement bonté qui ne resjouysse une nature bien née. Il y a certes je ne sçay quelle congratulation de bien faire qui nous resjouit en nous mesmes, et une fierté genereuse qui accompaigne la bonne conscience. Une ame courageusement vitieuse se peut à l'adventure garnir de securité, mais de cette complaisance et satisfaction elle ne s'en peut fournir. Ce n'est pas un leger plaisir de se sentir preservé de la contagion d'un siecle si gasté, et de dire en soy: Qui me verroit jusques dans l'ame, encore ne me trouveroit-il coulpable, ny de l'affliction et ruyne de personne, ny de vengence ou d'envie, ny d'offence publique des loix, ny de nouvelleté et de trouble,

> ny de faute à ma parole; et quoy que la licence du temps permit et apprinst à chacun, si n'ay-je mis la main ny és biens ny en la bourse d'homme François, et n'ay vescu que sur la mienne, non plus en guerre qu'en paix; ny ne me suis servy du travail de personne, says loyer. Ces tesmoignages de la conscience plaisent; et nous est grand benefice que cette esjouyssance naturelle, et le seul payement qui jamais ne nous manque. (III 2 807 B)

After citing the qualities which he most admires, Montaigne ironically terms order a dull and somber virtue. Thereupon he lists all the virtues associated with the household, and subsequently states that one must not be false to others or to oneself:

> Le peuple reconvoye celuy-là, d'un acte public, avec estonnement, jusqu'à sa porte: il laisse avec sa robbe ce rolle, il en retombe d'autant plus bas qu'il s'estoit plus haut monté; au dedans, chez luy, tout est tumultuaire et vile. Quand le reglement s'y trouveroit, il faut un jugement vif et bien trié pour l'appercevoir en ces actions basses et privées. Joint que l'ordre est une vertu morne et sombre. Gaigner une bresche, conduire une ambassade, regir un peuple, ce sont actions esclatantes. Tancer, rire, vendre, payer, aymer, hayr et converser avec les siens et avec soymesme doucement et justement, ne relácher point, ne se desmentir poinct, c'est chose plus rare, plus difficile et moins remerquable. Les vies retirées soustiennent par lá, quoy qu'on die, des devoirs autant ou plus aspres et tendus que ne font les autres vies. (III 2 809 B)

In other words, he feels that the primary virtue which man can possess is to know himself and to resist all attempts from without to force him to be untrue to what he believes. He writes that most people are content with the appearance of goodness rather than with that inward quality. Although he feels that true virtue lies in the coincidence of the inner and outer,

> (B) J'estime qu'au temple de Pallas, comme nous voyons en toutes autres religions, il y avoit des mysteres apparens pour estre montrez au peuple et d'autres mysteres plus secrets et plus hauts, pour estre montrés seulement à ceux qui en estoyent profez. Il est vray-semblable que en ceux icy se trouve le vray point de l'amitié que chacun se doibt. Non une science, la richesse et telles choses d'une affection principale

> et immoderée, comme membres de nostre estre, ny une amitié (B) molle et indiscrete, en laquelle il advient ce qui se voit au lierre, qu'il corrompt et ruyne la paroy qu'il accole; mais une amitié salutaire et reiglée, également utile et plaisante. Qui en sçait les devoirs et les exerce, il est vrayement du cabinet des muses; il a attaint le sommet de la sagesse humaine et de nostre bon heur. Cettuy-cy sçachant exactement ce qu'il se doibt, trouve dans son rolle qu'il doibt appliquer à soy l'usage des autres hommes et du monde, et, pour ce faire, contribuer à la société publique les devoirs et offices qui le touchent. (C) Qui ne vit aucunement à autruy, ne vit guere à soy. '*Qui sibi amicus est, scito hunc amicum omnibus esse.*' (B) La principale charge que nous ayons, c'est à chacun sa conduite; (C) et est ce pour quoy nous sommes icy. (B) Comme qui oublieroit de bien et saintement vivre, et penseroit estre quite de son devoir en y acheminant et dressant les autres, ce seroit un sot; tout de mesme, qui abandonne en son propre le sainement et gayement vivre pour en servir autruy, prent à mon gré un mauvais et desnaturé parti. (III 10 1006-1007)

many people are content with simply being known as virtuous: "...il se dict qu'il fait bon avoir bon nom, c'est à dire credit et reputation...." (I 46 276 A) But, in Montaigne's eye, virtue is its own reward—being good in itself, it thus requires no publicity:

> (C) Paul Aemile, allant en sa glorieuse expedition de Macedoine, advertit sur tout le peuple à Rome de contenir leur langue de ses actions pendant son absence. Que la licence des jugements est un grand destourbier aux grands affaires! D'autant que chacun n'a pas la fermeté de Fabius à l'encontre des voix communes, contraires et injurieuses, qui aima mieux laisser desmembrer son authorité aux vaines fantasies des hommes, que faire moins bien sa charge avec favorable reputation et populaire consentemant. (B) Il y a je ne sçay quelle douceur naturelle à se sentir louer, mais nous luy prestons trop de beaucoup. (II 16 625)

For many, however, virtue in itself is not enough. They want a fine reputation and will grovel before all for the sake of name and fame. Montaigne, in view of this perversion, deducts from the appraisal of the good deed the extent to which it is done for renown and with ostentation: "Qui que ce soit, ou art ou nature, qui nous imprime cette condition de vivre par la relation à autruy, nous faict beaucoup plus de mal que de bien. Nous nous defraudons de nos propres utilitez pour former les apparences à l'opinion commune. Il ne nous chaut pas tant quel soit nostre estre en nous et en effaict, comme quel il soit en la cognoissance publique. Les biens mesmes de l'esprit et la sagesse nous semble sans fruict, si elle n'est jouie que de nous, si elle ne se produict à la veuë et approbation estrangere.(III 9 955 B)

In contrast to virtue, Montaigne cites several types of vices, denouncing as he does the hypocrites who use euphemisms for vices: "Toutes sortes de nouvelle desbauche puisent heureusement en cette premiere et foeconde source, les images et patrons à troubler nostre police. On lict en nos loix mesmes, faites pour le remede de ce premier mal, l'aprentissage et l'excuse de toute sorte de mauvaises entreprises; et nous advient, ce que Thucidides dict des guerres civiles de son temps, qu'en faveur des vices publiques on les battisoit de mots nouveaux plus doux, pour leur excuse, abastardissant et amolissant leurs vrais titres. C'est, pourtant, pour reformer nos consciences et nos créances." (I 23 130 B)

Furthermore, he denounces those who betray others in belying their word of honor:

> Il y a des regles en la philosophie et faulses et molles. L'exemple qu'on nous propose, pour faire prevaloir l'utilité privée à la foy donnée, ne reçoit pas assez de poids par la circonstance qu'ils y meslent. Des voleurs vous ont prins, ils vous ont remis en liberté, ayant tiré de vous sermant du paiement de certaine somme; on a tort de dire qu'un homme de bien sera quitte de sa foy sans payer, estant hors de leurs mains. Il n'en est rien. Ce que la crainte m'a faict une fois vouloir, je suis tenu de le vouloir encore sans crainte; et quand elle n'aura forcé que ma langue sans la volontée encore suis je tenu de faire la maille bonne de ma parole. Pour moy, quand par fois ell'[*sic*] a inconsiderement devancé ma pensée, j'ay faict conscience de la desadvouer pourtant. Autrement, de degré en degré, nous viendrons renverser tout le droit qu'un tiers prend de nos promesses et sermens. '*Quasi vero forti viro vis possit adhiberi.*' (III 1 801 C)

He also believes that education should enhance one's existence, but that it becomes vicious if it does not:

> (C) Il ne dira pas tant sa leçon, comme il la fera. Il la repetera en ses actions. (A) On verra s'il a de la prudence en ses entreprises, s'il a de la bonté et de la justice en ses desportemens, (C) s'il a du jugement et de la grace en son parler, de la vigueur en ses maladies, de la modestie en ses

> jeux, de la tempérance en ses voluptez, (A) de l'indifference en son goust, soit chair, poisson, vin ou eau, (C) de l'ordre en son oeconomie: '*Qui disciplinam suam, non ostentationem scientiae, sed legem vitae putet, quique obtemperet ipse sibi, et decretis pareat*. (I 26 168)

He thus recommends that we live by our work, for our oaths and promises bind us. He feels this judgment to be valid for a prince as well, but he does allow one slight reservation here, preferring civil utility to honesty in the case of a ruler:

> (B) Le Prince, quand une urgente circonstance et quelque impetueux et inopiné accident du besoing de son estat luy faict gauchir sa parolle et sa foy, ou autrement le jette hors de son devoir ordinaire, doibt attribuer cette necessité à un coup de la verge divine: vice, n'est-ce pas, car il a quitté sa raison à une plus universelle et puissante raison, mais certes c'est mal'heur. De maniere qu'à quelqu'un qui me demandoit: Quel remede?—Nul remede, fis je: s'il fut veritablement geiné entre ces deux estremes (C) ('*sed videat ne quaeratur latebra perjurio*'), (B) il le falloit faire; mais s'il le fit sans regret, s'il ne luy greva de la faire, c'est signe que sa conscience est en mauvais termes. (III 1 799)

But in general he makes no exceptions. In his scale of values the word is important and should never be despised: "Si c'est grandeur de courage et l'effect d'une vertu rare et singuliere de mespriser l'amitié, les obligations privées, sa parolle et la parenté pour le bien commun et obeïssance du magistrat, c'est assez vrayement, pour nous en excuser, que c'est une grandeur qui ne peut loger en la grandeur de courage d'Epaminondas." (III 1 802 B) Such an admonition applies to all. It is thus deemed vicious to act solely on the basis of custom or tradition. In fact, the world tells us to put others above ourselves. Montaigne submits his father's dedication to public service as an example, but he reiterates that we should follow the dictates of our conscience rather than those of others.

This idea—to thine own self be true—is linked to the mask theme. Montaigne feels that too often people wish to appear otherwise than they are; therefore, they knowingly distort their true sentiments and adopt disguises: "C'est folie d'y attacher toutes ses pensées et s'y engager d'une affection furieuse et indiscrette. Mais, d'autre part, de s'y mesler sans amour et sans obligation de volonté, en forme de comediens, pour jouer un rolle commun de l'aage et de la coustume et n'y mettre du sien que les parolles, c'est de vray pourvoyer à sa seureté, mais bien láchement, comme celuy qui abandonneroit son honneur, ou son proffit, ou son plaisir, de peur du danger: car il est certain que, d'une telle pratique, ceux qui la dressent n'en peuvent esperer aucun fruict qui touche ou satisface une belle ame." (III 3 825 B) Along with misuse of truth, this is one of the worst vices according to Montaigne's system of moral evaluation. Honesty and hypocrisy are intimately related since Montaigne surmises that people are often not content to be themselves; they always feel they must hide behind masks or vain titles in order to gain acceptance.

The same link is also established between truth and personal integrity, for, on the moral plane, Montaigne feels that he does himself more harm by lying than he does the person about whom he is lying: "Je me fay plus d'injure en mentant, que je n'en fay à celuy de qui je mens." (II 17 659 B) To Montaigne's mind, lying is the worst of vices. A cowardly vice, it reveals a contempt for God and a fear of man: "C'est un vilein vice que le mentir, et qu'un ancien peint bien honteusement quand il dict que c'est donner tesmoignage de mespriser Dieu, et quand et quand de craindre les hommes." (II 18 666 A)

In general, with regard to religion, Montaigne believes that men are impudent in the way in which they bandy religion about:

> Sentez si ce n'est par noz mains que nous la menons, à tirer comme de cire tant de figures contraires d'une regle si droitte et si ferme. Quand c'est[*sic*] il veu mieux qu'en France en noz jours? Ceux qui l'ont prinse à gauche, ceux qui l'ont prinse à droitte, ceux qui en disent le noir, ceux qui en disent le blanc, l'employent si pareillement à leurs violentes et ambitieuses entreprinses, s'y conduisent d'un progrez si conforme en desbordement et injustice, qu'ils rendent doubteuse et malaisée à croire la diversité qu'ils pretendent de leurs opinions en chose de laquelle depend la conduitte et loy de nostre vie. Peut on veoir partir de mesme eschole et discipline des meurs plus unies, plus unes? (II 12 443 C)

This is no subject to be treated lightly or with irreverence. In addition, he questions the morality of civil insurrection for the sake of religion:

> Voyez l'horrible impudence dequoy nous pelotons les raisons divines, et combien irreligieusement nous les avons et rejettées et reprinses selon que la fortune nous a changé de place en ces orages publiques. Cette proposition si solenne: S'il est permis au subjet de se rebeller et armer contre son prince pour la defence de la religion, souvienne-vous en quelles bouches, cette année passée, l'affirmative d'icelle estoit l'arc-boutant d'un parti, la negative de quel autre parti

> c'estoit l'arc-boutant; et oyez à present de quel quartier vient la voix et instruction de l'une et de l'autre; et si les armes bruyent moins pour cette cause que pour cette là. Et nous bruslons les gents qui disent qu'il faut faire souffrir à la verité le joug de nostre besoing: et de combien faict la France pis que de le dire! (II 12 443 C)

On the whole, these statements reveal Montaigne's moral nature—his cult of virtue and his hatred of vice, particularly the hidden inner vice of hypocrisy which rends the human spirit asunder. He is concerned primarily with men's behavior, not with the content or the formulation of their philosophy. For Montaigne, morality is dependent on the values that man can evolve from daily life regarding what he can properly expect of himself while inhabiting an imperfect world.

What are the values of daily life and what is the role of language here? Such values are often founded in the integrity of the word. The truth of one's statements to one's fellows and to oneself are basic to daily intercourse. A knowledge of language and men is necessary to any formulation of value. Any man can appreciate the results of prevarication, but to appreciate its immediate presence requires an acknowledgement that language is often employed for an immediate end and that the meaning of yesterday will not suffice, and to appreciate the intention of the user of language requires continued involvement with men. The values of daily life may not alter significantly in reference to integrity and cilivization, but the composite world of their manifestation is a changing one.

The Virtuous Use of Language

Language and the Betrayal of Society

Montaigne judges the code of moral conduct of his day, and some of its precepts he finds wanting. However, he is no extremist. Hallie states: "The rules or prescriptions of society are our rules and prescriptions, as far as language, as far as law, as far as the institutions we are raised in are concerned; and if we fail to give them allegiance, we fail ourselves as well as them. We fail ourselves not only in the sense that our disorderly imaginations take the place of plain language and conscience, but also in the sense that we contribute by our neglect to the destruction of those institutions that keep us living in a peaceful community. Both inwardly and outwardly to betray or neglect society is to betray or neglect ourselves."[82]

Montaigne thus chooses not to subvert existing institutions; he simply wants men fully to understand themselves and to cease to be hypocritical concerning the discrepancy between public opinion and self-knowledge.

Certainly, he is not politically naive. He knows very well that a measure of dissimulation is necessary for politicians, but he feels that standards of truth may be somewhat stretched without being broken.

For Montaigne, the use of language is a moral issue: "Cet amoralisme rhétorique, dont il est question ici, se heurte non seulement aux principes de Platon mais aussi à ceux de Montaigne, pour qui la question de l'écriture se présente bien comme une question morale. L'enjeu en est bien la moralité, aussi bien au sens de l'opposition du bien et du mal, du bon et du mauvais, qu'au sens des moeurs, de la moralité publique et des bienséances sociales."[83].

As for religion and its effect on man's life, he holds out little hope for it to effect moral betterment: "Though his faith is sincere, his God is far above man's moral or intellectual reach, and apparently raises few men up by his extraordinary grace. The appalling practices of the time seem to prove that Christianity has little effect on conduct. What passes for it is a pretext for treachery and cruelty. Without any overt—perhaps even any conscious—break, Montaigne seems to ignore Christianity as he seeks a man-centered moral code that man has no excuse to infringe."[84]

And in seeking an anthropocentric code, Montaigne interrogates his own experiences and expresses them in the self-portrait; in so doing, he founds a moral code rooted in his own experiences, and in the end he comes to see self-study as a valid means for achieving knowledge of man in general and for developing an awareness—chronologically quite precocious—of human motivation. On the basis of a personal, individual psychology, he establishes a theory of human behavior foreshadowing the great theories of the latter century.

Language of Truth and Deceit: Hypocrisy on the Practical Level

In the first chapter disguise was discussed to show Montaigne's emphasis on learning about language and men—to be able to generalize about their nature. In this chapter, the emphasis is on the willful expression of truth—an ethical demand.

Emerging from Montaigne's psychological study of human behavior is the deep moral reprobation provoked in him by the uses evil men make of language. To Montaigne, the world is no stable, unchanging place in which one can depend on the truth of another's statements. In his age he sees too many instances of deceit and hypocrisy on a practical level for him to believe that the ideal of truth in human relationships is at all widespread. Of course, such a realization should not prevent him from upholding the ideal of truthfulness; and, as he often repeats, he believes that we learn more from the vices of others than from their virtues.

Consequently, he points out many instances in which people deceive one another. When he discusses peace conferences and treaties, for example, he states that they are often grounded in deceit: "Quand à nous, moings superstitieux, qui tenons celuy avoir l'honneur de la guerre, qui en a le profit, et qui apres Lysander, disons que où la peau du lion ne peut suffire, il y faut coudre un lopin de celle du renard, les plus ordinaires occasions de surprinse se tirent de cette praticque: et n'est heure, disons nous, où un chef doive avoir plus l'oeil au guet, que celle des parlements et traités d'accord." (I 5 26 A) The pragmatic Montaigne, well aware of human viciousness, avers that the parties of a treaty should not trust one another until the final seal has time to dry. His counsel to the unwary and innocent is to trust no one, and he gives an example of a situation in which people are killed unmercifully in express violation of a pact still in force: "Toutes-fois je vis dernierement en mon voisinage de Mussidan, que ceux qui en furent délogez à force par nostre armée, et autres de leur party crioient comme de trahison, de ce que pendant les entremises d'accord, et le traicté se continuant encores, on les avoit surpris et mis en pieces: chose qui eust eu à l'avanture apparence en un autre siecle. Mais, comme je viens de dire, nos façons sont entierement eloignées de ces reigles et ne se doit attendre fiance des uns aux autres, que le dernier seau d'obligation n'y soit passé: encore y a il lors assés affaire." (I 6 28 A) Another example of this type of deceit occurs in his relation of the drama involving the Counts of Horn and Egmont:

> Dernierement, en cette tragedie que le Duc d'Albe nous fit voir à Bruxelles ès Comtes de Horne et d'Aiguemond, il y eust tout plain de choses remarquables, et entre autres que ledict Comte d'Aiguemond, soubs la foy et asseurance duquel le Comte de Horne s'estoit venu rendre au Duc d'Albe, requit avec grand instance qu'on le fit mourir le premier: affin que sa mort l'affranchist de l'obligation qu'il avoit audict Comte de Horne. Il semble que la mort n'ait point deschargé le premier de sa foy donnée, et que le second en estoit quite, mesmes sans mourir. Nous ne pouvons estre tenus au delà de nos forces et de nos moyens. (I 7 30 A)

Furthermore, Montaigne regards haggling as an occasion of dissimulation: "J'excepte les payements où il faut venir à marchander et conter, car si je ne trouve à qui en commettre la charge, je les esloingne honteusement et injurieusement tant que je puis, de peur de cette altercation, à laquelle et mon humeur et ma forme de parler est du tout incompatible. Il n'est rien que je haisse comme à marchander. C'est un pur commerce de trichoterie et d'impudence: apres une heure de debat et de barquignage, l'un et l'autre abandonne sa parolle et ses sermens pour cinq sous d'amandement." (I 14 63 B)

But on a more personal level, Montaigne detects the same kind of behavior, whether it happens with respect to the communication between one man and another or within oneself. Here again the masqueraders are subjected to his relentless scrutiny, and his remarks are scathing. He thus attacks the deceit practiced in human communication: "Les Pythagoriens font le bien certain et finy, le mal infiny et incertain. Mille routtes desvoient du blanc, une y va. Certes je ne m'asseure pas que je peusse venir à bout de moy, à garantir un danger evident et extresme par une effrontée et solemne mensonge. Un ancien pere dit que nous sommes mieux en la compagnie d'un chien cognu qu'en celle d'un homme duquel le langage nous est inconnu. '*Ut externus alieno non sit hominis vice.*' Et de combien est le langage faux moins sociable que le silence." (I 9 37 B) Montaigne praises conscientiousness as a guarantee of truthfulness: "Je ne fay nul doubte qu'il ne creust ce qu'il escrivoit, car il estoit assez conscientieux pour ne mentir pas mesmes en se jouant," (I 28 194 A) but he adduces many other examples of men who make a practice of deception. For instance, he tells of a man who lies to himself and to everyone else about his religious belief: "Et celuy qui, se confessant à moy, me recitoit avoir tout un aage faict profession et les effects d'une religion damnable selon luy, et contradictoire à celle qu'il avoit en son coeur, pour ne perdre son credit et l'honneur de ses charges: comment patissoit-il ce discours en son courage? De quel langage entretiennent-ils sur ce subject la justice divine? Leur repentance consistant en visible et maniable reparation, ils perdent et envers Dieu, et envers nous le moyen de l'alleguer. Sont-ils si hardis de demander pardon sans satisfaction et sans repentance?" (I 54 320 C)

Furthermore, Montaigne feels that war gives rise to other forms of hypocrisy and dissimulation. The same travesty occurs when cowards seek to appear courageous: "On a raison de descrier l'hipocrisie qui se trouve en la guerre: car qu'est il plus aisé à un homme pratic que de gauchir aux dangers et de contrefaire le mauvais, ayant le coeur plein de mollesse? Il y a tant de moyens d'eviter les occasions de se hazarder en particulier, que nous aurons trompé mille fois le monde, avant que de nous engager à un dangereux pas; et, lors mesme, nous y trouvant empétrez, nous sçaurons bien pour ce coup couvrir nostre jeu d'un bon visage et d'une parolle asseurée, quoy que l'ame nous tremble au dedans." (II 16 625 A) This holds true as well with regard to his many examples of treachery. For instance, he speaks of individuals involved in treachery claiming that what they can not do honorably, they do expediently: "La justice requeroit que les Romains eussent raison de ce forfait; la difficulté en empéchoit les voyes ordinaires: ce qu'ils ne peurent legitimement sans guerre et sans hazard, ils entreprindrent de le faire par trahison. Ce qu'ils ne peurent honnestement, ils le firent utilement." (III 1 796 B) In Montaigne's moral universe perfidy may be excusable if it is used to punish perfidy.

In addition to human treachery and the difference between appearance and reality, the mutual polarity or coincidence of word and deed is another aspect of the mask theme exposed by Montaigne. In this regard, he depicts people who disguise their true thoughts by speaking with a forked tongue in order to gain a certain end. He advises these individuals to leave expediency to the Palace of Justice, for we basically offend ourselves when we lie. In essence, lies diminish the individual, and we lose our human dignity when we lie to save face or to bow to authority:

> De faute de prudence on retombe en faute de coeur, qui est encore moins supportable. La pluspart des accords de nos querelles du jourd'huy sont honteux et menteurs: nous ne cerchons qu'à sauver les apparences, et trahissons cependant et desadvouons nos vrayes intentions. Nous plastrons le faict: nous sçavons comment nous l'avons dict et en quel sens, et les assistans la sçavent, et nos amis, à qui nous avons voulu faire sentir nostre avantage. C'est aux despens de nostre franchise et de l'honneur de nostre courage que nous desadvouons nostre pensée, et cerchons des conillieres en la faucеté pour nous accorder. Nous nous desmentons nous mesmes, pour sauver un desmentir que nous avons donné. Il ne faut pas regarder si vostre action ou vostre parole peut avoir autre interpretation; c'est vostre vraie et sincere interpretation qu'il faut meshuy maintenir, quoy qu'il vous couste. On parle à vostre vertu et à vostre conscience; ce ne sont pas parties à mettre en masque. Laissons ces vils moyens et ces expediens à la chicane du palais. (III 10 1019 B)

Montaigne speaks further in a pejorative sense of self-deception as practiced by men of learning who read the Ancients and take credit for their ideas: "(B) Un president se vantoit, où j'estois, d'avoir amoncelé deux cens tant de lieux estrangers en un sien arrest presidental. (C) En le preschant à chacun il me sembla effacer la gloire qu'on luy en donnoit. (B) Pusillanime et absurde vanterie à mon gré pour un tel subject et telle personne." (III 12 1056) This theme also appears with reference to contemporary literature in which Montaigne detects much dissimulation. The same pejorative note is sounded in his discussion of titles and the false impression they create. Montaigne wonders what a title really means: "Il y a tant de liberté en ces mutations que, de mon temps, je n'ay veu personne, eslevé par la fortune à quelque grandeur extraordinaire, à qui on n'ait attaché incontinent des titres genealogiques nouveaux et ignorez à son pere, et qu'on n'ait anté en quelque illustre tige. Et, de bonne fortune, les plus obscures familles sont plus idoynes à falsification. Combien avons nous de gentilshommes en France, qui sont de Royalle race selon leurs comptes? Plus, ce croys-je, que d'autres." (I 46 278 B) It means of course nothing in itself: it is merely a word which tells us nothing about the person who bears it. In effect, the same is true of renown. People are foolish to seek recognition by the world, for such recognition is vain. Montaigne criticizes people who, usurping it for themselves, lay claim to another's reputation. Such individuals seek fame, not virtue: "C'est une piperie voisine à cettecy, d'appeller les offices de nostre estat par les titres superbes des Romains, encores qu'ils n'ayent aucune ressemblance de charge, et encores moins d'authorité et de puissance. Et cette-cy aussi, qui servira, à mon advis, un jour de tesmoignage d'une singuliere ineptie de nostre siecle, d'employer indignement, à qui bon nous semble, les surnoms les plus glorieux dequoy l'ancienneté ait honoré un ou deux personnages en plusieurs siecles." (I 51 307 A)

Montaigne finds that rulers turn this desire for good reputation among men against their subjects: "Puis que les hommes, par leur insuffisance, ne se peuvent assez payer d'une bonne monnoye, qu'on y employe encore la fauce," (II 16 629 C) for people may be contained by means of pseudo-opinions, and in politics the end quite often justifies the means. Frequently politicians make a habit of lying. As Montaigne states, a man who does not know how to lie does not know how to rule:

> Je ne sçay quelle commodité ils attendent de se faindre et contrefaire sans cesse, si ce n'est de n'en estre pas creus lors mesme qu'ils disent verité; cela peut tromper une fois ou deux les hommes; mais de faire profession de se tenir couvert, et se vanter, comme ont faict aucuns de nos princes, qu'ils jetteroient leur chemise au feu si elle estoit participante de leurs vrayes intentions (qui est un mot de l'ancien Metellus Macedonicus), qui ne sçait se faindre, ne sçait pas regner, c'est tenir advertis ceux qui ont à les practiquer, que ce n'est que piperie et mensonge qu'ils disent. (II 17 648 A)

This ironic statement is followed by one in which Montaigne admonishes rulers to employ this tactic sparingly. Inasmuch as people are not totally foolish, should they discover their masters' deviousness, they would no longer trust them: "Le gain qui les convie à la premiere desloyauté (et quasi toujours il s'en presente comme à toutes autres meschancetez: les sacrileges, les meurtres, les rebellions, les trahisons s'entreprenent pour quelque espece de fruit), mais ce premier gain apporte infinis dommages suivants, jettant ce prince hors de tout commerce et de tout moyen de negotiation par l'example de cette infidelité." (II 17 648 C) In addition, Montaigne sets forth his own standards in contrast to those of deceitful individuals. Above all else, he hates flattery, for he considers it one of the meanest forms of deception: "Par des richesses, on satisfaict les services d'un valet, la diligence d'un courrier, le dancer, le voltiger, le parler et les plus viles offices qu'on reçoive; voire et le vice s'en paye, la flaterie, le maquerelage, la trahison: ce n'est pas merveille si la vertu reçoit et desire moins volontiers cette sorte de monnoye commune, que celle qui luy est propre et particuliere, toute noble et genereuse. (II 7 382 A) In general terms, Montaigne extols classical virtue by way of contrast to the corruption of contemporary usage: "Il estoit bien esloigné de cette religion des anciens Romains, qui ne se vouloyent prevaloir en leurs guerres que de la vertu simple et nayfve; mais encore y apportoit il plus de conscience que nous ne ferions à cette heure, et n'approuvoit pas toutes sortes de moyens pour acquerir la victoire." (II 34 742 A) Discussing himself and his relationship to this idea, he once again speaks in more general terms of truth and deceit:

> (B) J'ay autresfois essayé d'employer au service des maniemens publiques les opinions et reigles de vivre ainsi rudes, neufves, impolies ou impollues, comme je les ay nées chez moy ou raportées de mon institution, et desquelles je me sers (C) sinon (B) commodéement (C) au moins seurement (B) en particulier, une vertu scholastique et novice. Je les y ay trouvées ineptes et dangereuses. Celuy qui va en la presse, il faut qu'il gauchisse, qu'il serre ses couddes, qu'il recule ou qu'il avance, voire qu'il quitte le droict chemin, selon ce qu'il rencontre; qu'il vive non tant selon soy que selon autruy, non selon ce qu'il se propose mais selon ce qu'on luy propose, selon le temps, selon les hommes, selon les affaires. (III 9 991)

Again Montaigne emphasizes this hatred of hypocrisy and dissimulation. Most men hide behind the mask; too many fear to speak the truth. Montaigne stresses his resolve to be faithful to his word above all else:

> (A) Car, quant à cette nouvelle vertu de faintise et de dissimulation qui est à cet heure si fort en credit, je la hay capitallement; et, de tous les vices, je n'en trouve aucun qui tesmoigne tant de lácheté et bassesse de coeur. C'est un humeur couarde et servile de s'aller desguiser et cacher sous un masque, et de n'oser se faire veoir tel qu'on est. Par là nos hommes se dressent à la perfidie: (B) estants duicts à produire des parolles fauces, ils ne font pas conscience d'y manquer. (A) Un coeur genereux ne doit desmentir ses pensées; il se veut faire voir jusques au dedans. (II 17 647)

In reviewing this catalog of Montaigne's ideas on truth and deceit, we find a man who rejects the mask, the lack of correspondence between word and deed. Ideally, he envisions a world rid of dishonesty, but, astute student of man that he is, he doubts the possibility of its realization. It is as though he detects some basic flaw in human nature, apparently irreparable, characterized by fear tinged with shame. This flaw finds expression in the passion to disguise oneself in order to win the approval of one's fellows. In Montaigne's own life he maintains sincerity no matter how dearly bought.

He believes in the beneficial potential of language and the reality of the honor and loyalty it fosters. Language, as we have previously stated, he identifies as the foundation of society. Montaigne will not place himself in moral jeopardy by perjuring himself. Certainly, as we have already mentioned, Montaigne is well aware of his penchant for exaggeration.

In the condemnation of his age, the purport of his work bears in large measure on the widespread practice of opportunistic, self-serving dishonesty: "Celuy qui faict tout pour l'honneur et pour la gloire, que pense-il gaigner en se produisant au monde en masque, desrobant son vray estre à la connoissance du peuple?" (III 5 847 B) Further contrasting truthfulness and lying, he writes the following: "(B) J'en voy qui estudient et glosent leurs Almanachs, et nous en alleguent l'authorité aux choses qui se passent. A tant dire, il faut qu'ils dient et la vérité et le mensonge: (C) '*Quis est enim qui totum diem jaculans non aliquando conlineet.*' (B) Je ne les estime de rien mieux, pour les voir tomber en quelque rencontre: ce seroit plus de certitude, s'il y avoit regle et verité à mentir tousjours." (I 2 43) But, in "Du démentir," Montaigne makes a sweeping statement relating lying and the era in which he lives. He claims that it is difficult to believe a person when he is speaking of himself, particularly since the first stage in the corruption of morals is dissimulation or lying. He believes that dissimulation is among the most notable qualities of the century:

> (A) Mais, à qui croyons nous parlant de soy, en une saison si gastée? veu qu'il en est peu, ou point, à qui nous puissions croire, parlant d'autruy, où il y a moins d'interest à mentir. Le premier traict de la corruption des moeurs, c'est le banissement de la verité: car, comme disoit Pindare, l'estre veritable est le commencement d'une grande vertu, et le premier article que Platon demande au gouverneur de sa republique. (A) Nostre verité de maintenant, ce n'est pas ce qui est, mais ce qui se persuade à autruy: comme nous appellons monnoye non celle qui est loyalle seulement, mais la fauce aussi qui a mise. Nostre nation est de long temps reprochée de ce vice: car Salvianus Massiliensis, qui estoit du temps de Valentinian l'Empereur, dict qu'aux François le mentir et se parjurer n'est pas vice, mais une façon de parler. Qui voudroit encherir sur ce tesmoignage, il pourroit dire que ce leur est à present vertu. On s'y forme, on s'y façonne, comme à un exercice d'honneur; car la dissimulation est des plus notables qualitez de ce siecle. (II 18 666)

It is apparent, then, that Montaigne views his age as one which encourages Machiavellianism. By implication, therefore, dissimulation flourishes in such a society. Such dissimulation is, as seen in the previous passage, a betrayal of society through language, for mutual understanding is reached by means of language. If one can not assume the truthfulness and sincerity of human intercourse, then the skeleton of the civil edifice, the basis of the social order, is cast aside. The extreme end of such a trend is chaos and the collapse of society. Thus Montaigne makes the following comparison: "Ce bon compaignon de Grece disoit que les enfans s'amusent par les osselets, les hommes par les parolles." (II 18 667 A)

Montaigne's pejorative comments on lying are aimed not only at society in general, but particularly at rulers of society, who may have recourse to dissimulation in order to win their people's trust. Once they have acceded to power, having no further use for dissimulation, they remove their masks and show their true selves, as for example in the case of Julius Caesar: "Pour revenir à sa clemence, nous en avons plusieurs naifs exemples au temps de sa domination, lors que, toutes choses estant reduites en sa main, il n'avoit plus à se feindre." (II 33 732 A)

Montaigne is very well aware that even good men may resort to hyperbole and deceit. As Starobinski puts it: "Le danger du mensonge et de l'hyperbole est donc inséparable de l'élan même de la parole, fût-ce chez un homme de bonne foi."[85] Montaigne's avowed horror of deceit leads him to think that he can sidestep this pitfall most of the time. He believes that human beings are bound to one another by their desire to keep their word in a given situation. He avers that truthful words are the cement of private life—our intelligence conducting itself by means of speech:

> (B) Moy-mesme, qui faicts singuliere conscience de mentir et qui ne me soucie guiere de donner creance et authorité à ce que je dis, m'apperçoy toutefois, aux propos que j'ay en main, qu'estant eschauffé (C) ou par la resistance d'un autre ou par la propre chaleur de la narration, (B) je grossis et enfle mon subject par voix, mouvemens, vigueur et force de parolles, et encore par extention et amplification, non sans interest de la verité nayfve. Mais je le fais en condition pourtant, qu'au premier qui me rameine et qui me demande la verité nue et crüe, je quitte soudain mon effort et la luy donne, sans exaggeration, sans emphase et remplissage. (C) La parole vive et bruyante, comme est la mienne ordinaire, s'emporte volontiers à l'hyperbole. (III 11 1028)

Starobinski concludes from the preceding passage the following: "Notre seul *être* possible joue sa chance dans la société de nos semblables, c'est-à-dire dans le monde du paraître. C'est pourquoi la parole véridique est tout ensemble le ciment de la vie publique et celui de notre identité privée."[86]

In his general commentary on lying, Montaigne makes the distinction between intentional and inadvertent lying,[87] and in essence he feels that all of us can fall into the second trap. However, the first category is the one which is most dangerous to society because it represents a deliberate appropriation of language to deceptive purposes. Montaigne ranges hypocrites in the latter category, and he sees the mask as a form of hypocrisy.

Overall, Montaigne is opposed to lying on ethical grounds, for men have only their words to relate them to other men. If these prove false, communication fails, and man is stranded in a world in which it is impossible to distinguish reality from illusion, a world peopled by hypocrites and liars who do not envision society as a body to be shielded from the fatal blows dealt by falsehood and pharisaism.

Always Montaigne insists that action is more important than meaningless words: "Montaigne was doing more than just paying lip-service to an ethical banality about words and deeds. His primary concern was not that man *ought* to act as he thought; he was convinced that an idea which was not tested in action was useless, and this testing had to be consciously attempted."[88]

In essence, then, when Montaigne studies man and his actions, he finds no order, no authentic connection between what he says and what he does. He finds that to many appearance is more important than reality and that words become tools of the mask.

On a moral level Montaigne attacks lying and perjury as contemptible and slavish: "Montaignes erste Einwände sind moralischer Natur: in Form subjektiv geäußerter und daher nur umso[*sic*] stärker überzeugender Urteile unterstreicht er das Verächtliche und Sklavische in Lüge und Vertrauensbruch."[89] He believes that deceit is evil in itself and that its repercussions are to be felt in both language and life. In addition, however, he feels that on a pragmatic level deceit ultimately fails its practitioners insofar as subjects eventually discover their rulers' treachery. And on the level of everyday life, Montaigne believes the same principle to apply; for eventually the liars, flatterers, and hypocrites appear in their true light: the mask can not succeed indefinitely in concealing an individual's true nature. Since he sees language as essential to life, his attitude toward man is influenced by the use which he feels men have made of language. He sees the world as a shifting, constantly changing entity, and he sees that the spurious use of language is a definite evil to society and a transgression against both nature and the social order.

> Language, like man himself, is a product of a long history of influences and activities for Montaigne, and it is tantamount to insanity to act as if this were not the case. The 'rule or

> prescription' of ordinary talk is something quite similar to the rules or customs of human society with regard to morality and religion. To violate them, to act in flat disregard of these rules or prescriptions in matters of language, is as dangerous to our thinking, Montaigne says throughout the *Essays*, as revolution and immorality are dangerous to society. All such radically new departures are not really independent of the past; they are *violations* of it, and as such they entail chaos and punishment. In our talk, in our thinking, we are as much involved with our past and with society as we are in morality and religion. In fact, customs and laws do not exist in society apart from our language and thinking; they inhabit and inform that language and thinking, at least if we would communicate with others; and when language breaks down, so does social order.[90]

In this sense, then, Montaigne's world is peopled by amoral individuals whose hypocrisies are unmasked by his words. In his world, the innocent are few; the evil predominate; and he turns language against them as they have turned it against others.

Why the emphasis on lying? Because this is a conscious decision to confuse reality, the nature of which is nebulous enough already. Men's efforts should be directed toward a continuing definition and its complexity rather than toward exploitation of it, for the simplest of reasons: the continuance of all that civilized behavior suggests in the intellectual, political, and esthetic realms. Such a judgment of the direction of men's efforts appears rational, but it is more particularly ethical. Men must attempt to define reality intellectually and philosophically, but the ethical demand is toward its willful expression in society.

Integrity and the Language of Innocence and Belief

In any discussion of Montaigne's conception of a type of language bespeaking moral innocence, we must bear in mind that innocence is apparently a rare quality among members of civilized society. In point of fact, Montaigne's comments on innocence are always limited to the presence of that quality in members of a primitive society or an ancient culture. He thereby suggests the lack of innocence among people of his own era and social class.

In "Si le chef d'une place assiegée doit sortir pour parlementer," he refers to a kind of language which has retained its pristine innocence. And in the passage in which he alludes to the South American Indians, he lauds their society for its innocence and want of treachery. In effect, he states: "(A) Les paroles mesmes qui signifient le mensonge, la trahison, la dissimulation, l'avarice, l'envie, la detraction, le pardon, inouies. Combien trouveroit il la republique qu'il a imaginée, esloignée de cette perfection: (C) *'viri a diis recentes.'* (B) *Hos natura modos primum dedit.*" (I 31 206-207)

In addition to the Indians' basic innocence, he thus praises their boldness and courage, and he states that they can be favorably compared to the ancient Greeks and Romans. It is apparent, then, that Montaigne admires this quality and that he wishes its adoption by his fellow men. However, the eminently pragmatic Montaigne realizes that such innocence is lost to his own society and that there is virtually no possibility that people of his era will ever possess that kind of innocence. We might even hazard to affirm that in Montaigne's view a civilized society foregoes innocence to the degree that the Indians possess it.

Since Montaigne himself appears to exist in a world in which he finds little which is innocent and just, it is natural that he would regard religious faith and those who profess it with a somewhat jaundiced eye. He searches through his world and in his reading for examples of people who are brave and courageous in defending their beliefs. For instance, he mentions the following episode: "Nous lisons de ceux de la ville d'Arras lors que le Roy Loys unziesme la print, qu'il s'en trouva bon nombre parmy le peuple qui se laisserent pendre, plustost que de dire: "Vive le roy." (I 14 32 A) Montaigne also mentions with admiration the South American Indian prisoners, for they are a people who put courage above the threat of execution. In so doing, they rob the victor of his spoils since there is no victory unless the vanquished foe concedes mastery: "Ils ne demandent à leurs prisonniers autre rançon que la confession et recognoissance d'estre vaincus; mais il ne s'en trouve pas un, en tout en siecle, qui n'ayme mieux la mort que de relascher, ny par contenance, ny de parole, un seul point d'une grandeur de courage invincible: il ne s'en void aucun qui n'ayme mieux estre tué et mangé, que de requerir seulement de ne l'estre pas." (I 21 210 A)

Furthermore, on the same subject, Montaigne alludes to devotees who are compelled to retract dogma under pressure:

> Or ce qui me semble aporter autant de desordre en nos consciences, en ces troubles où nous sommes, de la religion, c'est cette dispensation que les Catholiques font de leur creance. Il leur semble faire bien les moderez et les entenduz, quand ils quittent aux adversaires aucuns articles de ceux qui sont en debat. Mais, outre ce, qu'ils ne voyent pas quel avantage c'est à celuy qui vous charge, de commancer à luy ceder et vous tirer arriere, et combien cela l'anime à poursuivre sa pointe, ces articles là qu'ils choisissent pour les plus legiers, sont aucunefois tres-importans. Ou il faut se submettre du tout à l'authorité de nostre police ecclesiastique,

> ou du tout s'en dispenser. Ce n'est pas à nous à establir la part que nous luy devons d'obeïssance. (I 27 181-182 A)

And finally, mentioning names and religious belief, he alludes ironically to the Reformation: "Item, dira pas la posterité que nostre reformation d'aujourd'huy ait esté delicate et exacte, de n'avoir pas seulement combatu les erreurs et les vices, et rempli le monde de devotion, d'humilité, d'obëissance, de paix et de toute espece de vertu, mais d'avoir passé jusque à combatre ces anciens noms de nos baptesmes, Charles, Loys, François, pour peupler le monde de Mathusalem, Ezechiel, Malachie, beacoup mieux sentans de la foy? (I 46 277 A)

Many of Montaigne's other asseverations concerning faith deal directly with his own era or assume the form of historical anecdotes allegorically reflecting contemporary French events. An example of the latter occurs when Montaigne alleges the example of individuals who are forbidden to acknowledge that their gods had once been human: "Les Aegyptiens, d'une imprudente prudence, defendoyent sur peine de la hart que nul eust à dire que Serapis et Isis, leurs Dieux, eussent autres fois esté hommes; et nul n'ignoroit qu'ils ne l'eussent esté." (II 12 517 C)

But as to his own age, Montaigne holds that people are often deceitful even in prayer. According to Montaigne, faith should be verbalized by the conscience rather than by the tongue. Often when he sees people praying, he feels that their outward demeanor gives their words the lie: "(A) Toutesfois nous appellons Dieu et son ayde au complot de nous[*sic*] fautes, (C) et le convions à l'injustice. (B) *Quae, nisi seductis, nequeas committere divis.* (A) L'avaricieux le prie pour la conservation vaine et superflue de ses thresors; l'ambitieux, pour ses victoires et conduite de sa passion, le voleur l'employe à son ayde pour franchir le hazart et les difficultez qui s'opposent à l'execution de ses meschantes entreprinses, ou le remercie de l'aisance qu'il a trouvé à dégosiller un passant." (I 56 323-324) Montaigne probably sympathizes on this score with Stilpon, for whom religious belief and ritual is a private matter: "Stilpon le philosophe, interrogé si les Dieux s'esjouïssent de nos honneurs et sacrifices: Vous estes indiscret, respondit il: retirons nous à part, si vous voulez parler de cela." (II 12 523 C) In addition, again exploring contemporary society, Montaigne criticizes men who take advantage of religion by alleging divine authorization for their pronouncements: "Car, pour exemple, qu'est-il plus vain que de vouloir deviner Dieu par nos analogies et conjectures, le regler et le monde à nostre capacité et à nos loix, et nous servir aux despens de la divinité de ce petit eschantillon de suffisance qu'il luy a pleu despartir à nostre naturelle condition? Et, par ce que nous ne pouvons estendre nostre veuë jusques en son glorieux siege, l'avoir ramené ça bas à nostre corruption et à nos miseres? (II 12 512-513 A)

In Montaigne's judgment, religion for many is but words stripped of meaning; thus citing the Protestant translation of the Bible, he declares:

> Ce n'est pas l'estude de tout le monde, c'est l'estude des personnes qui y sont vouées, que Dieu y appelle. Les meschans, les ignorans s'y empirent. Ce n'est pas une histoire à compter, c'est une histoire à reverer, craindre, et adorer. Plaisantes gens, qui pensent l'avoir rendue maniable au peuple, pour l'avoir mise en langage populaire! Ne tient-il qu'aux mots qu'ils n'entendent tout ce qu'ils trouvent par escrit? Diray-je plus? Pour l'en approcher de ce peu, ils l'en reculent. L'ignorance pure et remise toute en autruy estoit bien plus salutaire et plus sçavante que n'est cette science verbale et vaine, nourrice de presomption et de temerité. (I 56 321 C)

In Montaigne's eye prayer casts a faint gleam of the divine upon mankind's benighted understanding—provided, of course, that it is heartfelt. Ritual and ceremony lend themselves to the growth of the religious spirit and are to be welcomed in that sense: "La majesté divine s'est ainsi pour nous aucunement laissé circonscrire aux limites corporels: ses sacremens supernaturels et celestes ont des signes de nostre terrestre condition; son adoration s'exprime par offices et paroles sensibles; car c'est l'homme, qui croid et qui prie." (II 12 513-514 C)

It is apparent that these attitudes toward faith reflect Montaigne's comprehensive attitude toward man's use of language: it is only man's misuse of prayer which is evil.

In Montaigne's condemnation of his age, its increasing dissimulation and sophistication, its loss of innocence, there is the conclusion that as far as ethics is concerned, men seem to be flawed with a passion to disguise the self. Language retains an innocent nature only in primitive or ancient cultures. How can the language of experience and sophistication speak of faith and belief? The language itself is corrupt and the innocent so few that prayer uttered by the faithful becomes suspect. An ongoing sophistication in language and the decision to employ it ethically become the essential components of the survival of society.

The religious spirit, it is assumed, is positive and based on goodness and virtue. The particular religion is unimportant; Montaigne deals with various cultures. It is the heartfelt adherence to beliefs reflected in action which is paramount. Language can do little to define the mysterious, but if its use in prayer is obviously sincere and reflective of belief, it may have a beneficial effect.

Montaigne's intellectual and philosophical inquiries into the nature of knowledge and reality and their relationships to language and psychology yield a particularly Renaissance and Montanean skepticism and relativism. The implications of that necessarily ongoing inquiry for the practical day-to-day existence of men in society are primarily ethical. Moral behavior cannot be maintained by anything less than continued sophistication in the processes of political and professional exploitation of man's multi-intentional self and his so accurately reflective language.

The dependence of the ethical upon the intellectual is therefore considerable. However, as the mind may be rational though not ethical, society becomes dependent upon the *willful* expression of truth. This implies truth to oneself, based in knowledge of oneself, truth to one's fellows based in the knowledge that the innocent are few, and integrity in language is based in the realization that language is as corrupt or innocent as those who employ it.

The ideal of truth in human relationship upon which the state is founded, upon which society depends—while not widespread—must not be discarded. There is an ethical burden upon the responsible individual, and it is reflected in his understanding and use of language.

CHAPTER III

The Language Of Esthetic Action: The Appearance Of Truth

Freedom and Boldness in the Self-Portrait

Spontaneity: The Denial of Prohibition in the Use of Language

In the first chapter we have seen Montaigne as thinker, his mind ordering and attempting to depict the universe on an intellectual and philosophical level. In the second chapter we saw Montaigne the man, a unique human being living and acting in the world, determining the ethical application of language. In the third chapter we will see Montaigne as an artist exercising his taste in the province of literature, determining the components of beauty in the use of language. Here his senses and judgment come into play, and his esthetic is delineated.

Montaigne often took a stand against existing conventions, and one of the major contemporary conventions was the taboo interdicting certain terminology. Montaigne, who, as we have seen, carefully distinguished between language and its referent, thought such prohibition absurd. The syllogism resuming his ideational development respecting spontaneity might be thus abridged: if a thing exists, it is natural, and anything natural should be expressed through language regardless of the custom of the day. Pertile expresses Montaigne's conception concerning the relationship between thought and language in an enlightening fashion: "Dagli esempi dati, si capisce che l'opinione di Montaigne è per certi aspetti diversa da quella di Cicerone. Infatti, mentre questi vuole limitare il campo del pensabile, Montaigne vuole estendere al massimo quello del dicibile: si deve cioè poter dire tutto ciò che si pensa, e non, come sostiene l'oratore latino: si deve pensare solo ciò che si può dire."[91]

Without hesitation, Montaigne characterizes himself as fulfilling his diplomatic role by speaking frankly and boldly: "En ce peu que j'ay eu à negotier entre nos Princes, en ces divisions et subdivisions qui nous deschirent aujourd'huy, j'ay curieusement evité qu'il[*sic*] se mesprinssent en moy et s'enferrassent en mon masque. Les gens du mestier se tiennent les plus couverts, et se presentent et contrefont les plus moyens et les plus voisins qu'ils peuvent. Moy, je m'offre par mes opinions les plus vives et par la forme plus mienne." (III 1791 B) Pursuing this idea he avers that he is always true to himself and that he avoids false impressions. There is no self-interest involved here, for he refrains from saying nothing which spontaneously occurs to him:

> Tendre negotiateur et novice, qui ayme mieux faillir à l'affaire qu'à moy!...La naifveté et la verité pure, en quelque siecle que ce soit, trouvent encore leur opportunité et leur mise....Messieurs, ne considerez pas si je suis libre, mais si je le suis sans rien prendre et sans amender par là mes affaires. Ma liberté m'a aussi aiséement deschargé du soubçon de faintise par sa vigueur (n'espargnant rien à dire pour poisant et cuisant qu'il fut, je n'eusse peu dire pis, absent et qu'elle a une montre apparente de simplesse et de nonchalance. Je ne pretens autre fruict en agissant, que d'agir, et n'y attache longues suittes et propositions: chasque action fait particulierement son jeu: porte s'il peut. (III 1 791-792 B)

He extends this theme by stating that he is not prudent in expressing himself. He cares only to say what he thinks: "Aussi que j'ay naturellement peine à me communiquer à demy et avec modification, et cette servile prudence et soupçonneuse qu'on nous ordonne en la conversation de ces amities nombreuses et imparfaictes; et nous l'ordonne l'on principalement en ce temps, qu'il ne se peut parler du monde que dangereusement ou faucement." (III 3 821 B)

He claims that such is not always the case, for writers suppress information in writing history. They do not relate everything; tendentiously, they simply relate the events which will best support their own point of view: "On peut couvrir les actions secrettes; mais de taire ce que tout le monde sçait, et les choses qui ont tiré des effects publiques et de telle consequence, c'est un defaut inexcusable." (II 10 420 A)

Furthermore, he judges unfavorably the attitude of his age toward sex and the use of certain words defining bodily functions. According to Montaigne, people are squeamish about using certain words: "...il faut laisser aux femmes cette vaine superstition des parolles...." (I 49 298 A) He also criticizes his era for its attitudes toward sexual language. He claims that although people may converse freely of murder and other atrocities, discussing sex is forbidden. He feels that this kind of bashfulness is an ornament to youth, but a reproach to old age: "Qu'a faict l'action genitale aux hommes, si naturelle, si necessaire et si juste, pour n'en oser parler sans vergnongne et pour l'exclurre des propos serieux et reglez? Nous prononçons hardiment: tuer, desrober, trahir; et cela, nous n'oserions qu'entre les dents? Est-ce à dire que moins nous en exhalons en parole, d'autant nous avons loy d'en grossir la pensée?" (III 5 847 B)

According to Montaigne's point of view, language ought not to be fraught with ludicrous taboos. As Parslow stated: "To Montaigne this concealment of the truth is a perfect symbol of language being used as if the bodily actions of its users were on one planet and the words on another. The fact is that bodily actions are the very life of language."[92]

Accordingly, such an evaluation may also comprise Montaigne's predilection for the natural, coarse language of soldiers, for theirs is a language without pretense: "It is the language of men talking with men, and it deals with hidden parts of the body unashamedly, just as it deals with sex."[93] As for women, Montaigne believes that they are hypocritical, for "...in public they are too afraid to talk about what they are not at all afraid to do in private—the sexual act, defecation, and such."[94]

This aspect of Montaigne became more accentuated as he revised his earlier writings. In essence, he distinguished man's comic aspects and his eternal struggle to maintain his dignity. The strength of his language and his use of obscenities wax as his sense of man's clay feet increases.[95] His literary conception of language—a universal concern for language as an expression of the totality of human experience, committing to posterity the lofty as well as the base aspects of his character—shares with his conception of the use of language in the intellectual and ethical spheres a passion for sincerity and integrity.

Characteristics of the Spontaneous: Creating an Efficacious Style

The same Montaigne who saw the comic and base aspects of man also saw himself as part of man. As Traeger points out, he sees all sides of a question; the resultant inconclusiveness, which might seem a weakness, is in fact a strength: "Aber dann ist das 'Ich' der Selbstaussage nicht mehr nur Montaigne, sondern ein Vertreter menschlichen Denkens überhaupt. Und die Schwäche, nicht entscheiden zu können, weil Gründe and Gegengründe in gewissen Fragen gleiche Kraft haben, ist die Stärke, über den Gründen die Gegengründe nicht zu vergessen. Montaignes Selbstkritik erscheint höchst ambivalent."[96] But perhaps his strength does, in fact, lie in this quality as well. He set out to portray himself, and thus his ability to see all sides makes his portrait complete if somewhat confusing. As was pointed out earlier, it is difficult to determine when he is criticizing himself with tongue-in-cheek and when he is not, but even his deliberate self-deprecation may point the way to some truth about him, and often his self-criticism becomes a form of disguised self-portrait.

Montaigne tells us that he prefers grave and austere matters, and he claims that he has a formless and undisciplined way of talking. He is often dull, earnest, and unentertaining. He justifies this by saying that he adopts a humble and popular way of speaking, lacking in ease or polish because he wishes to avoid affectation:

> (A) Tout est grossier chez moy; il y a faute de gentillesse et de beauté. Je ne sçay faire valoir les choses pour le plus que ce qu'elles valent, ma façon n'ayde rien à la matiere. Voilà pourquoy il me la faut forte, qui aye beaucoup de prise et qui luise d'elle-mesme. (C) Quand j'en saisis des populaires et plus gayes, c'est pour me suivre à moy qui n'aime point une sagesse ceremonieuse et triste, comme faict le monde, et pour m'esgayer, non pour esgayer mon stile, qui les veut plustost graves et severes (au moins si je dois nommer stile un parler informe et sans regle, un jargon populaire et un proceder sans definition, sans partition, sans conclusion, trouble, à la guise de celuy d'Amafanius et de Rabirius. (II 17 637)

Although there is a self-criticism in this section, Montaigne appears to feel that his "natural" way of speaking is actually the best way of expressing himself, and he appears to be praising his style for its lack of affectation. Also, he claims that he could do better speaking than writing: "(A) Au demeurant, mon langage n'a rien de facile et poly: il est aspre (C) et desdaigneux, (A) ayant ses dispositions libres...je suy tout simplement ma forme naturelle: "d'où c'est à l'adventure que je puis plus à parler qu'à escrire." (II 17 638)

Furthermore, he claims to write only at home—where his work is often interrupted by the necessity of travel—and to make very few corrections: (A) "Ce fagotage de tant de diverses pieces se faict en cette condition, que je n'y mets la main que lors qu'une trop lasche oisiveté me presse, et non ailleurs que chez moy. Ainsin il s'est basty à diverses poses et intervalles, comme les occasions me detiennent ailleurs par fois plusieurs moys. Au demeurant, je ne corrige point mes premieres imaginations par les secondes; (C) ouy à l'aventure quelque mot, mais pour diversifier, non pour oster." (II 37 758) On the other hand, he praises his own style by saying that his indirect manner of expressing himself is stylistically excellent. He wishes to surpass the commonplace in order to reach words of flesh and bone:

> Nos gens appellent jugement, langage; et beaux mots, les plaines conceptions. Cette peinture est conduitte non tant par dexterité de la main comme pour avoir l'object plus vifvement empreint en l'ame. Gallus parle simplement, par ce qu'il conçoit simplement. Horace ne se contente point d'une superficielle expression, elle le trahiroit. Il voit plus cler et plus outre dans la chose; son esprit crochette et furette tout le magasin des mots et des figures pour se représenter; et les luy

> faut outre l'ordinaire. Plutarque dit qu'il veid le langage latin par les choses; icy de mesme: le sens esclaire et produict les parolles; non plus de vent, ains de chair et d'os. (III 5 873 B)

Laughing at himself, he chides the flow of babble which emanates from his pen: "Pour finir ce notable commentaire, qui m'est eschappé d'un flux de caquet, flux impetueux par fois et nuisible..." (III 5 897 B) And he excuses his flaws by insisting that he does not wish to make writing his profession: (B) Si j'eusse voulu parler par science, j'eusse parlé plustost: j'eusse escript du temps plus voisin de mes estudes, que j'avois d'esprit et de memoire; et me fusse plus fié à la vigueur de cet aage là qu'à cettuy-icy, si j'en eusse voulu faire mestier (C) d'escrire." (III 12 1056-1057) Moreover, he appears to criticize at length his writing and style:

> Cette farcisseure est un peu hors de mon theme. Je m'esgare, mais plustot par licence que par mesgarde. Mes fantasies se suyvent, mais par fois c'est de loing, et se regardent, mais d'une veuë oblique. (C) J'ay passé les yeux sur tel dialogue de Platon mi party d'une fantastique bigarrure, le devant à l'amour, tout le bas à la rhetorique. Ils ne creignent point ces muances, et ont une merveilleuse grace à se laisser ainsi rouler au vent, ou à le sembler. (B) Les noms de mes chapitres n'en embrassent pas tousjours la matiere; souvent ils la denotent seulement par quelque marque.... (III 9 994)

But by and large, despite his critical statements and his seemingly false modesty, Montaigne is unmistakably proud of the *Essais* and is convinced of the efficacy of his style. He contends that the content and meaning of his work are great and that elegance is unimportant when balanced against this quality. He also claims to have some ability in writing letters and imparts the qualities of his style thus:

> Pour en ranger davantage, je n'en entasse que les testes. Que j'y attache leur suitte, je multiplieray plusieurs fois ce volume. Et combien y ay-je espandu d'histoires qui ne disent mot, lesquelles qui voudra esplucher un peu ingenieusement, en produira infinis Essais. Ny elles, ny mes allegations ne servent pas toujours simplement d'exemple, d'authorité ou d'ornement. Je ne les regarde pas seulement par l'usage que j'en tire. Elles portent souvent, hors de mon propos, la semence d'une matiere plus riche et plus hardie, et sonnent à gauche un ton plus delicat, et pour moy qui n'en veux exprimer d'avantage, et pour ceux qui rencontreront mon air.

> Revenant à la vertu parliere, je ne trouve pas grand choix entre ne sçavoir dire que mal, ou ne sçavoir rien que bien dire. '*Non est ornamentum virile concinnitas.* (I 40 251 C)

As critics have to a great extent dismissed his false modesty and self-criticism, so does Thibaudet assert that Montaigne has put himself on trial in language as well as in character.[97] In general Thibaudet eulogizes Montaigne's style: "Tous les tours et toutes les grâces du français naturel. Une prose transparente qui va du langage le plus naïf à la poésie la plus légère et au trait le plus concis. Aucun clavier plus riche dans la langue."[98] Regosin agrees, commenting appreciatively on Montaigne's use of physical, concrete, and real words: "What good and useful writings do, he tells us, is to set the language, to pin it down in time....The words become fixed as the man is portrayed and, we understand, the man assumes being through the words."[99] In fact, for Regosin, Montaigne reaches a "...new level of language in attempting to portray himself."[100] He feels that although Montaigne uses old words, he redefines certain words and concepts, making them more controlled: "He seeks a language of resolution where word and being merge...and...goes beyond metaphor to evoke another level of cognition."[101] Lablénie enlarges this concept, stating that although Montaigne did not wish to be known as a writer he speaks constantly of the art of writing:

> Montaigne, qui a méprisé le métier d'écrivain, parle constamment de son art d'écrire. Soit directement, soit indirectement, à travers les opinions qu'il exprime sur les autres auteurs, tout au long des *Essais* il porte des jugements sur son livre, son but, ses conceptions, sa composition, son style, sa langue....Sous les contradictions apparentes, le lecteur retrouvera sans difficulté l'unité d'une pensée ferme et nuancée: Bien écrire, c'est suivre du plus près possible le cours d'une idée qui traduit les expériences, les 'essais' d'une vie. L'art est au service de la vie, de la nature. Comme son sens l'indique, il ne doit être qu'adaptation. Plus il s'adapte, plus il s'efface; plus il s'efface, meilleur il est. Mais c'est là que réside la difficulté. Il tend toujours à transparaître. Et il faut en définitive beaucoup travailler pour savoir rester, devenir, ou redevenir naturel.[102]

In point of fact, Montaigne was of course an artist. He was a shrewd observer of human nature and life in general; this was abetted by his innately curious nature. His word, with its conversational style, is effective in communicating the breadth and scope of his mind, and although he speaks of disorder in his writing, his writing takes its order from the very character which shaped it. Above all, he was an individual who respected truth and sincerity and who hated the hypocrisy which excludes communication between men.

As Baraz puts it: "Fort peu d'oeuvres expriment l'unité de l'homme de façon aussi parfaite que les *Essais* de Montaigne: la pensée y apparaît seulement en tant qu'activité du moi, et le moi y est décrit comme étant en train de penser pour 'se regler'; bien plus, ils expriment cette unité par leur forme littéraire autant que par leur contenu."[103]

Art and Effectiveness in Language

Appraising the Ancients

Montaigne, sharply critical of his own work, was thus aware of the qualities of literature in general, whether contemporary or classical. He had a strong esthetic sense and marked well the character of literary excellence.

In particular, as his writing reveals, he had a great reverence for the Ancients and for the beauty they created: "Mais cela n'oste rien du goust à ceux qui ont bon nez, ny ne desroge à la gloire de ces anciens autheurs qui, comme il est vraysemblable, mirent premierement ces mots en ce lustre." (III 5 874 B) He felt that content was important in any work, and he makes this observation concerning Tacitus' work: "Ce n'est pas un livre à lire, c'est un livre à estudier et apprendre; il est si plain de sentences qu'il y en a à tort et à droict: c'est une pepiniere de discours ethiques et politiques, pour la provision et ornement de ceux qui tiennent rang au maniement du monde." (III 8 941 B) He also praises Amyot's translation of Plutarch, stating:

> Je donne avec raison, ce me semble, la palme à Jacques Amyot sur tous nos escrivains François, non seulement pour la naïfveté et pureté du langage, en quoy il surpasse tous autres, ny de son sçavoir, ayant peu développer si heureusement un autheur si espineux et ferré (car on m'en dira ce qu'on voudra: Je n'entens rien au Grec, mais je voy un sens si beau, si bien joint et entretenu par tout en sa traduction que, ou il a certainement entendu l'imagination vraye de l'autheur, ou, ayant par longue conversation planté vivement dans son ame une generale Idée de celle de Plutarque, il ne luy a aumoins rien presté qui le desmente ou qui le desdie); mais sur tout je lui sçay bon gré d'avoir sçeu trier et choisir un livre si digne et si à propos, pour en faire present à son pays. (II 4 363 A)

In addition, he compares the books of the Ancients to those of the moderns, saying that the former are fuller and stronger than the latter which tend to be simply entertaining: "Si ce livre me fasche, j'en prens un autre; et ne m'y addonne qu'aux heures où l'ennuy de rien faire commence à me saisir. Je ne me prens guiere aux nouveaux, pour ce que les anciens me semblent plus pleins et plus roides...." (II 10 409-410 A) Montaigne very much admires the purity and polish of Caesar's language: "Mais Caesar singulierement me semble meriter qu'on l'estudie, non pour la science de l'histoire seulement, mais pour luy mesme, tant il a de perfection et d'excellence par dessus tous les autres, quoy que Saluste soit du nombre." (II 10 416 A) And he makes further favorable comments on the writings of a medieval historian: "En mon Philippe de Comines il y a cecy: Vous y trouverez le langage doux et aggreable, d'une naifve simplicité; la narration pure, et en laquelle la bonne foy de l'autheur reluit evidemment, exempte de vanité parlant de soy, et d'affection et d'envie parlant d'autruy." (II 10 419 A) In addition, he points out the difficulties inherent in translating the grace and eloquence of language. He stresses in contrast the relative facility of working with a logical treatise: "(A) Or, quelques jours avant sa mort, mon pere, ayant de fortune rencontré ce livre soubs un tas d'autres papiers abandonnez, me commanda de le luy mettre en François. Il faict bon traduire les autheurs comme celuy-là, où il n'y a guiere que la matiere à representer; mais ceux qui ont donné beaucoup à la grace et à l'elegance du langage, ils sont dangereux à entreprendre: (C) nommément pour les rapporter à un idiome plus foible." (II 12 439-440)

Mentioning specific qualities which he admires, Montaigne makes further meliorative comments on writers. For example, he believes that fertility of thought is important in enriching language, and he compares several ancient cultures in light of this quality: "Les Atheniens (dict Platon) ont pour leur part le soing de l'abondance et elegance du parler; les Lacedemoniens, de la briefveté, et ceux de Crete, de la fecundité des conceptions plus que du langage: ceux-cy sont les meilleurs." (I 26 172-173 A) Once again stressing his celebrated opposition between eloquence and wisdom, words and deeds, Montaigne reaffirms his preference. He contends, however, that perfection consists in the possession of both qualities, such as was the achievement of Cicero: "Et, outre cette difference, encore ne sont ce pas lettres vuides et descharnées, qui ne se soutiennent que par un delicat chois de mots, entassez et rangez à une juste cadence, ains farcies et pleines de beaux discours de sapience, par lesquelles on se rend non plus eloquent, mais plus sage, et qui nous apprennent non à bien dire, mais à bien faire. Fy de l'eloquence qui nous laisse envie de soy, non des choses; si ce n'est qu'on die que celle de Cicero, estant en si extreme perfection, se donne corps elle mesme." (I 40 252 A)

As to Plato, his comments are distinctly complimentary. Citing several verses of Lucretius, Montaigne praises his beautiful language: "Voylà des paroles tresmagnifiques et belles...." (II 12 489 A) In commenting further on the Ancients, he speaks of their sincerity, emphasizing that a man who says what he authentically believes arrests our attention:

> Oyez Cicero parler de l'amour de la liberté, oyez en parler Brutus: les escrits mesmes vous sonnent que cettuy-cy estoit homme pour l'acheter au pris de la vie. Que Cicero, pere d'eloquence, traite du mespris de la mort; que Seneque en traite aussi: celuy là traine languissant, et vous sentez qu'il vous veut resoudre de chose dequoy il n'est pas resolu; il ne vous donne point de coeur, car luy-mesmes n'en a point; l'autre vous anime et enflamme. Je ne voy jamais autheur, mesmement de ceux qui traictent de la vertu et des offices, que je ne recherche curieusement quel il a esté. (II 31 716 A)

In the foregoing catalog of Montaigne's laudatory comments on other authors, he apprises us of the qualities he admired in his own writing and in the writing of others. Eloquence, coherence, beauty, grace—all these qualities are for Montaigne the cachets of fine prose; these are the qualities he seeks to emulate in his own writing.

In Montaigne's serious concern with writing as an art, he also made numerous pejorative remarks concerning writers and style. For example, accusing them of unseemly and distasteful ambition, he criticizes Pliny and Cicero for having published their private correspondence: "Mais cecy surpasse toute bassesse de coeur, en personnes de tel rang, d'avoir voulu tirer quelque principale gloire du caquet et de la parlerie, jusques à y employer les lettres privées écriptes à leurs amis: en maniere que, aucunes ayant failly leur saison pour estre envoyées, ils les font ce neantmoins publier avec cette digne excuse qu'ils n'ont pas voulu perdre leur travail et veillées." (I 40 249 A)

He likewise calls to account the custom of using long harangues, titles, and formulas in letters:

> Comme j'ayme mieux composer deux lettres que d'en clorre et plier une, et resigne tousjours cette commission à quelque autre: de mesme, quand la matiere est achevée, je donrois volontiers à quelqu'un la charge d'y adjouster ces longues harengues, offres et prieres que nous logeons sur la fin, et desire que quelque nouvel usage nous en descharge; comme aussi de les inscrire d'une legende de qualitez et tiltres, pour ausquels ne broncher, j'ay maintesfois laissé d'escrire, et notamment à gens de justice et de finance. Tant d'innovations d'offices, une si difficile dispensation et ordonnance de divers noms d'honneur, lesquels, estant si cherement acheptez, ne peuvent estre eschangez ou oubliez sans offense. Je trouve pareillement de mauvaise grace d'en

> charger le front et inscription des livres que nous faisons imprimer. (I 40 253-254)

Furthermore, he criticizes Aretino's turgid style:

> Platon a emporté ce surnom de divin par un consentement universel, que aucun n'a essayé luy envier; et les Italiens, qui se vantent, et avecques raison, d'avoir communément l'esprit esveillé et le discours plus sain que lés autres nations de leur temps, en viennent d'estrener l'Aretin, auquel, sauf une façon de parler bouffie et bouillonnée de pointes, ingenieuses à la vérité, mais recherchées de loing et fantasques, et outre l'eloquence en fin, telle qu'elle puisse estre, je ne voy pas qu'il y ait rien au dessus des communs autheurs de son siecle; tant s'en faut qu'il approche de cette divinité ancienne. Et le surnom de grand, nous l'attachons à des Princes qui n'ont rien au dessus de la grandeur populaire. (I 51 307 A)

The doctrinaire nature of other literature also comes under attack when he derides it for chewing our morsels for us: "Ceux d'entredeux (qui est la plus commune façon, ceux la nous gastent tout: ils veulent nous mascher les morceaux; ils se donnent loy de juger, et par consequent d'incliner l'histoire à leur fantasie: car, dépuis que le jugement pend d'un costé, on ne se peut garder de contourner et tordre la narration à ce biais." (II 10 417 A)

In general, then, it can be seen that Montaigne is appalled by a Ciceronian style with its protracted and tedious approach to eloquence. As Thibaudet pointed out, Montaigne was particularly opposed to the Ciceronian style because he sees language as an ever-changing vehicle; therefore, he feels that "...s'attacher aux mots, c'est s'attacher à ce qui s'écoule, et se démode."[104] Nolan also reiterates this point, claiming that Montaigne's comments concerning Cicero are largely satiric.[105]

It is also possible to say that Montaigne was opposed to all writing which was ostentatious and verbose[106] and that he opposed intemperance of invention.[107] Thibaudet further states that "Les livres de son temps sentent pour lui le rance et le moisi."[108] Indeed Montaigne makes disparaging comments concerning all writing which was not natural and simple in style. In this, as in all else, he hated pretense, and he felt that the verbose, erudite style of the scholar and the pedant was false and hypocritical and that, in itself, such a style constituted an esthetic as well as a moral violation of language.

Precision, Dialect, and Decorum

Certainly, Montaigne's personal and esthetic evaluation of languages and dialects is closely connected to his literary criticism, since he saw literature in terms of its employment of language—which is also, of course, to see its moral complement. In languages and dialects he searched for the same qualities that he looked for in examining and evaluating literature.

In literature, he admires the beauty and precision of language, and the same is true for his comments on a given language. He says, "(A) Il y a bien au dessus de nous, vers les montaignes, un Gascon, que je treuve singulierement beau, sec, bref, signifiant, et à la verité un langage masle et militaire plus qu'autre que j'entende; (C) autant nerveux, puissant et pertinant, comme le François est gratieus, delicat et abondant." (II 17 639) In addition, he suggests that we surmount the commonplace in studying foreign languages: "...en Italie, je disois ce qu'il me plaisoit en devis communs; mais, aus propos roides, je n'eusse osé me fier à un idiome que je pouvois plier ny contourner outre son alleure commune." (III 5 873 B) He believed that knowledge of Greek and Latin was acquired for too dear a price: "C'est un bel et grand agencement sans doubte que le Grec et Latin, mais on l'achepte trop cher." (I 26 173 A) Furthermore, he makes laudatory comments on the softness of the language of the New World natives and on the beauty of its desinences: "Leur langage, au demeurant, c'est un doux langage et qui a le son aggreable, retirant aux terminaisons Grecques." (I 31 213 A)

By and large, his most numerous esthetic judgments on languages are reserved for jargon. Exposing its emptiness, he decries it thus: "Je ne sçay s'il en advient aux autres comme à moy; mais je ne me puis garder, quand j'oy nos architectes s'enfler de ces gros mots de pilastres, architraves, corniches, d'ouvrage Corinthien et Dorique, et semblables de leur jargon, que mon imagination ne se saisisse incontinent du palais d'Apolidon, et, par effect, je trouve que ce sont les chetives pieces de la porte de ma cuisine." (I 51 307 A)

Furthermore, in Montaigne's view, language is an ever-changing phenomenon which adapts itself to each new era. Of his own language he writes: "J'escris mon livre à peu d'hommes et à peu d'années. Si ç'eust esté une matiere de durée, il l'eust fallu commettre à un langage plus ferme. Selon la variation continuelle qui a suivy le nostre jusques à cette heure, qui peut esperer que sa forme presente soit en usage, d'icy à cinquante ans?" (III 9 982 B) Because he felt that language, as it existed in his own day, was in the process of rapid change, aptness or pertinency of content of speech is an abiding concern:

> Isocrates l'orateur, estant prié en un festin de parler de son art, chacun trouve qu'il eut raison de respondre: Il n'est pas maintenant temps de ce que je sçay faire; et ce dequoy il est maintenant temps, je ne le sçay pas faire. Car de presenter des harangues ou des disputes de rhetorique à une compaignie assemblée pour rire et faire bonne chere, ce seroit un meslange de trop mauvais accord. (I 26 164 A)

Overall, then, Montaigne's comments on languages and dialects emphasize the natural and simple rhythms of ordinary speech. He describes Latin and its effect on his writing and discusses dialects.[109] In addition, he observes that language escapes our grasp and a fixed language helps "...to pin it down in time...."[110] He also sets down rules for the use of colloquialism.[111] He valued brevity and coherence, and he attributed beauty to language endowed with these qualities.

In addition to Montaigne's comments concerning the beauty and precision of certain languages and dialects and his opinions of jargon, he also spoke of the necessity of using language appropriate to specific occasions, one example of which we have just discussed.

Quite often, Montaigne believed, men misuse language in this sense. For example, he tells of the orator talking about his art at a gathering whose purpose is pure pleasure. In that case, the orator's rhetorical language is out of place. And he makes the distinction here between people who are able to use the language and those able to analyze it: "Il ne sçait pas ablatif, conjunctif, substantif, ny la grammaire; ne faict pas son laquais ou une harangiere du petit pont, et si vous entretiendront tout vostre soul, si vous en avez envie, et se desferreront aussi peu, à l'adventure, aux regles de leur langage, qui le meilleur maistre és arts de France. Il ne sçait pas la rhetorique, ny pour avant-jeu, capter la benivolence du candide lecteur, ny ne luy chaut de le sçavoir. De vray, toute cette belle peincture s'efface aisément par le lustre d'une vérité simple et naifve." (I 26 169 A) Proceeding tangentially, he asserts his fondness for puns: "'*Pungit dolor*? *Vel fodiat sane. Si nudus es, da jugulum*; *sin tectus armis Vulcaniis, id est fortitudine, resiste*'; et ce mot des Grecs convives qu'ils y appliquent: '*Aut bibat aut abeat.*' (qui sonne plus sortablement en la langue d'un Gascon qui change volontiers en V le B, qu'en celle de Cicero)...." (II 12 496 C)

To Montaigne, bombastic language was appropriate for lawyers, the masses, schools, heralds, and the courts: "Ny les subtilitez grammairiennes, ny l'ingenieuse contexture de parolles et d'argumentations n'y servent; je veux des discours qui donnent la premiere charge dans le plus fort du doubte: les siens languissent autour du pot. Ils sont bons pour l'escole, pour le barreau et pour le sermon, où nous avons loisir de sommeiller, et sommes encore, un quart d'heure apres, assez à temps pour rencontrer le fil du propos." (II 10 414 A)

Often people mistake judgment for language; Montaigne feels, however, that a certain kind of language—preferably terse and entertaining—is appropriate for a conversation at a banquet: "Varro demande cecy au convive: l'assemblée de personnes belles de presence et agreables de conversation, qui ne soyent ny muets ny bavards, netteté et delicatesse aux vivres et au lieu, et le temps serain." (III 13 1106 B)

As for Montaigne himself, he is beguiled by Latin, enjoying the language tremendously: "Les polices, les moeurs loingtaines me flattent, et les langues; et m'appercoy que le latin me pippe à sa faveur par sa dignité, au delà de ce qui luy appartient, comme aux enfans et au vulgaire." (II 17 634 C) He thus claims to use whatever language lends itself most readily to the occasion at hand.

Language is affected by circumstance. It is evident from his comments and a study of his work as a whole that Montaigne believed that we alter our language to befit place, time, our interlocutors, and the occasion. As Thibaudet stated: "Non seulement il parle à Paris un langage autre qu'à Montaigne, mais il parle autrement."[112] As it stands for him, so for others, and language thus evolves. As Starobinski said,

> Montaigne, d'abord, revendique sa liberté, il veut se 'désaliéner', et à cette fin, il lui faut rompre des liens multiples,—liens qui constituent la situation de fait (réseaux de la coutume, de l'opinion, des autorités instituées, etc.) dans laquelle le philosophe se découvre captif avant de s'éveiller à la réflexion; mais, faisant effort pour se ressaisir, pour se définir, pour penser sa 'vraie nature', il postule par sa libre parole de nouveaux liens, il en appelle à des consciences étrangères qui sont, cette fois, passées au rang d'interlocuteurs, de lecteurs, de public; et, du même coup il en arrive à reconnaître la légitimité relative de la première dépendance—l'homme ne se conçoit pas hors d'une société civile—et il peut désormais rendre justice à ces 'liens artificiels', à ces 'usages' dont il s'était d'abord dégagé comme d'une servitude. Il peut alors y revenir librement, y emprunter ce qui lui convient: les inflexions vigoureuses du langage familier proviennent de cette région....[113]

The Pretense of Bombast and Grandiloquence

As much as Montaigne disliked anything, he hated the pretense and vanity of bombastic language. It was to him another kind of hypocrisy, one used to conceal feeble and illogical arguments and which contradicted all his basic convictions concerning style.

In this instance, he speaks of royal language with all its foolish ostentation, describing it as an empty, vain use of language: "Personne n'est exempt de dire des fadaises. La malheur est de les dire curieusement. *Nae iste magno conatu magnas nugas dixerit.* Cela ne me touche pas. Les miennes m'eschappent aussi nonchallamment qu'elles le valent. D'où bien leur prend. Je les quitterois soudain, à peu de coust qu'il y eust. Et ne les achette, ny les vens que ce qu'elles poisent. Je parle au papier comme je parle au premier que je rencontre. Qu'il soit vray, voicy dequoy." (III 1 790 B) For Montaigne, some language contains more sound than sense. This is particularly true of the work of poetasters. He feels that the latter create nothing new and are satisfied hypocritically taking credit for a work they have not themselves created: "Tite Live dict vray, que le langage des hommes nourris sous la Royauté est tousjours plein des folles ostentations et vains tesmoignages: chacun eslevant indifferemment son Roy à l'extreme ligne de valeur et grandeur souveraine." (I 3 16 C) Montaigne reiterates this point when, referring to Cicero, he speaks of being smothered by long-winded prefatory remarks. In this case he feels this language utterly lacks substance. This may be good for the schools, but is certainly not to his liking: "Quant à Cicero, les ouvrages qui me peuvent servir chez luy à mon desseing, ce sont ceux qui traitent de la philosophie signamment morale. Mais, à confesser hardiment la verité (car, puis qu'on a franchi les barrieres de l'impudence, il n'y a plus de bride), sa façon d'escrire me semble ennyeuse[*sic*], et toute autre pareille façon. Car ses prefaces, definitions, partitions, etymologies, consument la plus part de son ouvrage; ce qu'il y a de vif et de mouelle, est estouffé par ses longueries d'apprets." (II 10 413 A)

Once again he makes a pejorative allusion to the same fault and berates individuals who use language in which content is lacking. Ironically he asks: "Irois-je alterer à l'eloquence son parler?" (II 12 543 C)

Furthermore, Montaigne continues to develop this theme when he points out that no one is exempt from saying silly things, but that the horror of such a bagatelle is that many say foolish things with great seriousness: "Personne n'est exempt de dire des fadaises. Le malheur est de les dire curieusement." (III 1 790 B) He also reproves writers fond of a manner in which words obnubilate meaning: "L'eloquence faict injure aux choses, qui nous destourne à soy." (I 26 172 C)

In addition to his comments on bombast in general, Montaigne makes strong pejorative statements about specific writers given to grandiloquent prose: "Comme aux accoustremens c'est pusillanimité de se vouloir marquer par quelque façon particuliere et inusitée: de mesmes, au langage, la recherche des frases nouvelles et de mots peu cogneuz vient d'une ambition puerile et pedantesque." (I 26 172 C)

It can be deduced from this catalog of Montaigne's comments on bombast that he, by implication, was indicating the characteristics he admired in the use of language. He wanted language to be integral: "Montaigne a le sentiment d'un art fait de choses solides, contre le verbalisme, le trait, l'enflure."[114] He envisioned it as a manifestation conveying human emotions and thought in a simple, natural manner. He hated the practice of saying little and using many words to do so; thus it is that his esthetic judgment took umbrage at this extremely common practice. In addition, his sentiments in this matter are closely allied to the moral and philosophical revulsion he unleashed upon hypocrites and liars. Bombastic language could only lead to distrust and to a collapse of communication. Moreover, language, when trimmed with brevity and coherence, was much admired by him on an esthetic as well as on a moral and philosophical plane; therefore, its opposite, bombastic language, was soundly and unequivocally derided.

Brevity and Coherence

Montaigne's comments, then, on brevity and coherence appear to directly contrast with his deprecatory statements concerning pomposity. Much can be accomplished by suggestion. He particularly emphasizes this point when he states that brevity is more important than padding. His praise of brevity is based on the idea that it leaves readers desirous of more rather than that they should be drowned in words devoid of meaning: "(A) Il [Plutarch] sçavoit qu'és choses bonnes mesmes on peut trop dire, et que Alexandridas reprocha justement à celuy qui tenoit aux Ephores des bons propos, mais trop longs: O estrangier, tu dis ce qu'il faut, autrement qu'il ne faut. (C) Ceux qui ont le corps gresle, le grossissent d'embourrures: ceux qui ont la matiere exile, l'enflent de paroles." (I 26 157) Of himself, he says that when committing his thoughts to pen and paper, as soon as he begins to draw them out, he is no longer there: "Celles qui me coustent le plus sont celles qui valent le moins: depuis que je les traine, c'est signe que je n'y suis pas. Je commence volontiers sans project; le premier traict produict le second. Les lettres de ce temps sont plus en bordures et prefaces, qu'en matiere." (I 40 253 B) He speaks further of his ideal of achieving coherence and brevity in his own work. He esteems brevity but declines to arrogate it to himself: he belittles himself in comparison to Seneca and Plutarch:

> (A) Mais je sens bien que par fois je m'y laisse trop aller, et qu'à force de vouloir eviter l'art et l'affectation, j'y retombe d'une autre part: *brevis esse laboro, Obscurus fio*. (C) Platon dict que le long ou le court ne sont proprietez qui ostent ny donnent prix au langage. (A) Quand j'entreprendroy de suyvre cet autre stile aequable, uny et ordonné, je n'y sçaurois advenir; et encore que les coupures et cadences de Saluste reviennent plus à mon humeur, si est-ce que je treuve Caesar et plus grand et moins aisé à representer; et si mon inclination me porte plus à l'imitation du parler de Seneque, je ne laisse pas d'estimer davantage celuy de Plutarque. (II 17 638)

As mentioned above, Montaigne prefers a certain Gascon dialect for its brevity and concision: "(A) Il y a bien au dessus de nous, vers les montaignes, un Gascon, que je treuve singulierement beau, sec, bref, signifiant, et à la verité un langage masle et militaire plus qu'autre que j'entende; autant nerveux, puissant et pertinant, comme le François est gratieus, delicat et abondant." (II 17 639)

Moving from his own writing to that of others, he makes several appreciative comments about other authors. For example, as previously mentioned, he admires the French translation of Plutarch for its coherence.

Overall, then, we can see that Montaigne's admiration addresses itself to writers who have mastered the art of writing beautifully honed prose. It is this use of language which is proper according to his esthetic theory, and such is the style which he attempts to emulate in his own work.

The Language of Poetry

Beauty and the Ethereal: Rhythm and Idea

Of all forms of writing, Montaigne's most favorable esthetic and artistic remarks are reserved for poetic language. It is here that he sees language shedding its earth-bound forms and soaring into the ethereal realm of the spirit. In point of fact, he even speaks of Plato's poetic language, appropriately enough in a strikingly poetic metaphor: "Voyez prendre à mont l'essor à Platon en ses nuages poetiques; voyez chez luy le jargon des Dieux." (II 12 544 C) In this sense, considering his intense awe of authentic poetic language, he chides those who only mimic great poetry. He says that people who copy poetry are copying only the sound; they achieve naught but poor imitations of the original beauty of the poem: "(A) Depuis que Ronsard et du Bellay ont donné credit à nostre poésie Françoise, je ne vois si petit apprentis qui n'enfle des mots, qui ne renge les cadences à peu près comme eux. (C) *Plus sonat quam valet.*" (A) Pour le vulgaire, il ne fut jamais tant de poétes. Mais, comme il leur a esté bien aisé de representer leurs rithmes, ils demeurent bien aussi court à imiter les riches descriptions de l'un et les delicates inventions de l'autre." (I 26 171) Of Homer, Montaigne writes: "A cette cause le peut on nommer le premier et dernier des poëtes, suyvant ce beau tesmoignage que l'antiquité nous a laissé de luy, que, n'ayant eu nul qu'il peut imiter avant luy, il n'a eu nul apres luy qui le peut imiter. Ses parolles, selon Aristote, sont les seules parolles qui ayent mouvement et action; ce sont les seuls mots substantiels." (II 36 753 A) In effect, he feels that poetry is more than right rhythm, for rhythm alone does not create poetry: "Je ne suis pas de ceux qui pensent la bonne rithme faire le bon poeme: Laissez luy allonger une courte syllabe, s'il veut; pour cela, non force; si les inventions y rient, si l'esprit et le jugement y ont bien faict leur office, voylà un bon poete, diray-je, mais un mauvais versificateur." (I 26 170 A) And his esthetic judgment is frankly affronted by the poetasters, for he states: "Mille poëtes trainent et languissent à la prosaïque..." (III 9 995 B) In addition, in a condescending tone, he speaks of the amusing poetry with its pretty use of words which is suitable for women. He allows it a purpose, but it certainly is not great poetry: "Avec cette science, elle[*sic*] commandent à baguette et regentent les regens et l'eschole. Si toutesfois il leur fache de nous ceder en quoy que ce soit, et veulent par curiosité avoir part aux livres. La poësie est un amusement propre à leur besoin: c'est un art follastre et subtil, desguisé, parlier, tout en plaisir, tout en montre, comme elles." (III 3 823 B)

On the other hand, he finds that pleasing poetical language possesses euphony: "Or j'ay assez de commerce avec la poësie pour juger cecy, que non seulement il n'y a rien de barbarie en cette imagination, mais qu'elle est tout a fait anacreontique. Leur langage, au demeurant, c'est un doux langage et qui a le son aggreable, retirant aux terminaisons Grecques." (I 31 213 A) He also believes that poetry is enhanced by being recited. He holds that recitation has a great deal to do with the interpretation of a poem, and he digresses here to address himself to the esthetics of recitation:

> (B) Quant à moy, je ne m'estime point assez fort pour ouyr en sens rassis des vers d'Horace et de Catulle, chantez d'une voix suffisante par une belle et jeune bouche. (C) Et Zenon avoit raison de dire que la voix estoit la fleur de la beauté. On m'a voulu faire accroire qu'un homme, que tous nous autres François cognoissons, m'avoit imposé en me recitant des vers qu'il avoit faicts, qu'ils n'estoient pas tels sur le papier qu'en l'air, et que mes yeux en feroyent contraire jugement à mes oreilles, tant la prononciation a de credit à donner prix et façon aux ouvrages qui passent à sa mercy. (II 12 593)

Above all, Montaigne conceives poetry, which is unashamedly metaphoric in suggestion and association, as lifting man above the ordinary, removing him from the static terror and tedium of trivia.

The Amplitude of the Poetic

According to Regosin, Montaigne believed that poetry is a surrogate for physical love, but all in all a poor substitute. "Montaigne bemoans the absence of physical love and indicates poetry's potential as surrogate....Fully conscious that literature is a poor substitute for love-making, Montaigne can appreciate what it does bring him..."[115] Montaigne writes: "Elle represente je ne sçay quel air plus amoureux que l'amour mesme. Venus n'est pas si belle toute nue, et vive, et haletante, comme elle est icy chez Virgile...." (III 5 849 B)

Commenting on Montaigne's concepts concerning the use of metaphor in poetry, Regosin further states: "Through the creation of metaphor, the talented mind calls up new associations and relationships, new realities. It bends, stretches and twists language, giving it body and texture, and the language, thus living, acts upon the reader."[116] Montaigne also says that the sense of the poem vivifies it, particularly since it signifies more than it expresses: "It is a central paradox of the *Essais* that the very words which transcribe being can give rise to ambiguities and variations which cloud the faces of that being. Montaigne's remark that words can mean more than they say points to both sides of this medal. Through the third book we see him moving toward a new level of language, one which reflects more directly the nature of his subject."[117] Butor also remarks Montaigne's thought with respect to the relation between poetry and existence: he notes Montaigne's contention that poetry is a means of fortifying oneself against death.[118]

Moreover, Lablénie says that Montaigne "...apprécie les libertés de la poésie...."[119] and that "Il [Montaigne] estime qu'il est difficile de la [la poésie] juger, parce qu'il lui arrive d'échapper aux règles de l'art...."[120] And finally, Conche points out that Montaigne believed that in philosophy was the original poetry, but that dogmatists have destroyed it.[121]

As can be seen from these critical pronouncements and from Montaigne's approving comments on poetry, he felt that poetry and its language represented the culmination of man's domination of the spirit and the human condition through language. In poetry, Montaigne saw the potentiality of man fulfilled, and although he found little great poetry, what he was able to descry encouraged his belief in the indestructibility of the essentially human spirit.

In the poetic there may be a freedom, a loosening of intellectual absolutism which is not so acceptable in prose, though Montaigne may have wished his *Essais* to be exceptional in this respect. This freedom, this peculiarly Montanean integrity of the relative—so amenable to the artistic, to the poetic, is akin to the brevity and conciseness he praises in any artful use of the language; and it is, of course, only the esthetic equivalence of sincerity in intellectual and ethical use of language.

CONCLUSION

Thus it is that there emerges from this study a variegated reportrayal of Montaigne's elucidation of language. There is no conclusion, in the sense that Montaigne clearly intended that there be none, but only an indefinitely continuing series of efforts (*Essais*) on the most crucial of the three planes heretofore discussed. This is of course the intellectual or philosophical which necessarily, in view of Montaigne's Pyrrhonist perspective, could only be purely speculative, could indeed pretend to no conclusion, in the sense of definition or determination, precisely because Montaigne was convinced of the intellectual futility of dogmatism or doctrinairism.

Montaigne's attempt is one toward communication, toward realization of the self and toward establishment of social order. It is an attempt at the integration of the intellectual, moral, and esthetic planes. Though skeptical as to the possibility of absolute truths, his "system" of thought, if one may so term it, is based on certain assumptions. It appears assumed that 1) a particular sort of human society is desirable; 2) the basic nature of language is organic; 3) sincerity is the foundation of civilized action; 4) a search for knowledge is not only satisfying, but is necessary; and 5) some truths of a relative sort, at least, may be ascertained about the nature of human action and motivation.

One of the less fortunate truths about man's nature becomes for Montaigne the crux of his attempt at coherence and integration. This is the recognition that innocence is lost and that there is virtually no possibility that the people of his era will ever possess it. Rather, one discovers the "doubleness" and deception that man practices upon his fellows and the resulting disintegration of those standards which allow a society of men to cohere. The nature of language enables it to serve man's dual nature—to control, to limit, or to free.

Civilized behavior is not to be defined necessarily in the realm of manners, but in the commitment of men to recognize the centrality of integrity; it is based on truthful communication and the ethical application of knowledge and language. Part of his emphasis upon *this* world is the requirement that man act courageously, even heroically. This involves not only the mere exertion of will, but an ethical exertion of the will. It involves a recognition by man not only of his imperfect moral nature, but also the recognition that his nature is reflected in language. It requires, that is, an heroic use of language.

If a thing can be named, name it precisly as one can; if it can not be, one is not to pretend precision where there can be none. To so confuse by language the ideal and the real, for example, is to reveal either a certain ignorance or, more likely, a contemptible hypocrisy employed for individual gain. To be courageous may be to adopt a most decorous usage of the language.

Precision may be hypocrisy in the realms of the supernatural and the beautiful; it may not be so on the ethical plane.

This reflection of the doctrine of the appropriate—the potential of language to reflect both reason and the spirit, the self and the selfless—requires one to use a language of poetry and prayer, of signification and the concrete. And to mix them with the utmost care. Deliberate confusion results in the abuse of language, the weakening of social order, and the debasing of one's ethical propensities.

Student of the classical heritage, Montaigne refused any sort of absolute commitment on the basic human endeavor, that of understanding. This is to his credit, inasmuch as in this regard he patently stands in opposition to virtually all of his contemporaries. Moreover, in the scope of the centuries elapsed, the justification of his stance has been more and more plainly vindicated. It is undeniably for this very reason that his unpretentious skepticism continues to endear him to new generations of readers. Indeed, in light of recent criticism, one may reasonably hope for a revival of interest in the Montanean world. Should this occur, it would be well to advise neophytes of the impossibility of circumscribing the intellectual heritage of Montaigne, for it is one, by its very nature, which successfully resists any such effort. By its very nature fraught with contradiction, anomaly, ambiguity, and paradox, it lends itself to ongoing and ceaseless speculation. An extremely clever personality and author, Montaigne was able to endow posterity with a document potentially poisonous to the social, political, and intellectual climates in which he himself was compelled to exist. Nevertheless, he was no amoralist. On the contrary, it is on the moral plane that he is most firm. Reprimanding the many abuses, the many transgressions of what he perceived to be the ideal, albeit unmistakably practical, code of human and humane conduct occurring during his watchful lifetime, he may rightly be qualified as a great practitioner and exponent of moral philosophy, an able and worthy descendant of the ancient greats whom he admired and loved.

Thus it is that the intellectual and moral planes are resolved, the former in Pyrrhonism, the latter in explicit determination. But what can be said of the third plane which we have sought to clarify and define? Montaigne esthete may be thought to assume an intermediary position with regard to the absolute and the relative. His own tastes and likings are definite, precise, and unmistakable; yet he allows for the existence of contrary or dissimilar appreciation on the part of others. Well aware that one may only presume upon oneself, punctiliously correct in the sense of his cherished "honnête homme," he categorically refuses the so-called divine conceit. He sets forth an enlightened as well as judicious criticism certainly unequalled in his era. His basic esthetic criterion is that of sincerity and simplicity.

Inimical to what may be generally termed tautology, he sagaciously and successfully eschewed its slightest manifestation in his life's work.

Relentlessly assailing its appearance elsewhere, and thus reinforcing the basic Hellenic esthetic assumption, he has transmitted to posterity a document peerless in his own and in the present age likewise.

The potential of language for non-meaning is also Montaigne's concern. The purpose of language is meaning, not rhetoric. It should be the servant of meaning and the vehicle of communication. But its very nature, its creation and subsequent independent existence, its cumulative meaning can have a life of its own. It becomes so unwieldy, so suggestive of a variety of meanings that a knowledge of men and language becomes indispensable to ethical behavior.

Montaigne's quite integral conception of human action, then, is intimately connected with a knowledge of the nature of language, with the operation of the intellect upon itself for philosophical, political, and esthetic ends. The operation of the ethical intellect requires that one inquire into the nature of the self and of men, that one develop a conception of reality and the nature of knowledge, and that one observe the role of language and its relation to ideas and human intentions. It is necessary that one apply such knowledge of man and his use of language to a conception of society, to ethical behavior, and to literary creation.

The qualities that Montaigne finds in literature are those that he emphasizes in any ethical approach to the use of the language. Freedom and boldness, which are the components of a spontaneity freed from slavish adherence to established authority and custom, a language of precision and brevity rather than bombast and grandiloquence are indicative of his concern with meaning and communication rather than obfuscation or deception. They reveal his conception of beauty, his esthetic analogue of ethical and intellectual truth.

The crucial aspect of the intellectual—the operation of unlimited intellect upon the discovery, creation, and analysis of knowledge—is that it must precede any attribution of value to life.

Only after the attainment of a conception of truth and reality—for Montaigne a continuing *process*—can one have the material for ethical action or artistic creation, not to speak of any sort of philosophical justification of man. The intellectual process is, for Montaigne, effected by his peculiar dialectical movement between the self and the world, which constituted his literary method—a purposeful process founded in his definition of truth's relative nature and based in the conclusion that neither life nor language exists in a condition of stasis.

It is, in conclusion, the commitment to the right relationship between eloquence and wisdom, words and deeds which inheres in Montaigne's conceptions of language. His views on the attempt to ascertain and state truths about the nature of the self in relation to society, his emphasis on the intimate connection among virtue, language and social order—the will to express truth—and finally, his declaration that integrity, truth, and sincerity are components of the esthetic—the appearance of truth—all serve to elucidate his conceptions of language.

NOTES

1. Wolf Eberhard Traeger, *Aufbau und Gedankenführung in Montaignes Essays* (Heidelberg: C. Winter, 1961).

2. Barbara C. Bowen, *The Age of Bluff: Paradox and Ambiguity in Rabelais and Montaigne* (Urbana: Univ. of Illinois Press, 1972).

3. Traeger, 171.

4. Bowen, 105.

5. Hugo Friedrich, *Montaigne* (Paris: Gallimard, 1968).

6. Richard Regosin, "Language and the Dialectic of the Self in Montaigne's *Essais*," *Kentucky Romance Quarterly* 19, suppl. no. 1 (1972): 167-75.

7. Dilys Veronica Winegrad, "Expression and Being and the *Essais* of Montaigne," (Ph.D. diss., University of Pennsylvania, 1970).

8. More precisely, the concepts expression and being define language; whereas theme and image describe it.

9. Dilys Veronica Winegrad, "Language as Theme and Image in the *Essais* of Montaigne," *Symposium* (Syracuse University), n.s., 28, 3 (fall 1974): 274.

10. The phrase Regosin uses to describe this synthesis is "language of resolution."

11. Hélène Hédy Ehrlich, *Montaigne: la critique et le langage* (Paris: Klincksieck, 1972).

12. Traeger, 275.

13. Ibid., 276.

14. Morris Parslow, "Montaigne's Composition: A Study of the Structure of the *Essays* of the Third Book," (Ph.D. diss., Princeton University, 1954), 67.

15. Donald M. Frame, *Montaigne: A Biography* (New York: Harcourt, Brace and World, 1965), 83.

16. Ibid.

17. Philip P. Hallie, *The Scar of Montaigne: An Essay in Personal Philosophy* (Middletown, Conn.: Wesleyan Univ. Press, 1966), 96.

18. Frame, 184.

19. Hallie, 97.

20. Jean Starobinski, "Montaigne en mouvement," *Nouvelle Revue Française* 8, 36 (janvier-mars 1960): 16.

21. Floyd Gray, *Le Style de Montaigne* (Paris: A.G. Nizet, 1958), 129.

22. Donald J. Nolan, "Montaigne's Use of the Comic in the *Essais*," (Ph.D. diss., University of Illinois, 1967), 134.

23. Gray, 67
24. Frame, 187.
25. Helmut A. Hatzfeld, "Per una definizione dello stile di Montaigne," *Convivium*, n.s., 3 (maggio-giugno 1954): 290.
26. Hallie, 101.
27. Parslow, 91.
28. Ibid., 89.
29. Ehrlich, 16-7.
30. Ibid., 20.
31. Bowen, 103.
32. Albert Thibaudet, *Montaigne* (Paris: Gallimard, 1963), 499.
33. Ibid.
34. Regosin, 174.
35. Ibid., 175.
36. Hallie, 103.
37. Marcel Conche, *Montaigne ou la conscience heureuse* (Paris: Séghers, 1966), 67.
38. Edmond Lablénie, *Essais sur Montaigne* (Paris: Société d'édition d'enseignement supérieur, 1967), 115.
39. Pierre Moreau, *Montaigne*, 5th ed., (Paris: Hatier, 1958), 44.
40. Nolan, 154.
41. Ibid.
42. Traeger, 21.
43. Ibid., 127.
44. Ibid., 147.
45. Ibid., 167.
46. Ehrlich, 20.
47. Ibid.
48. Parslow, 55.
49. Bowen, 114-5.
50. Frame, 293.
51. Ibid., 187.
52. Ibid.
53. Bowen, 104.
54. Ibid., 109.
55. Hallie, 113.
56. Ehrlich, 72.
57. Giacomo Tauro, *Montaigne* (Milan: Società editrice Dante Alighieri di Albrighi, Segati & c., 1928), 207.
58. Frame, 198.
59. Tauro, 183.
60. Regosin, 169.

61. Ibid., 170.
62. Cf. ibid., 174.
63. Friedrich, 133.
64. Ibid., 129.
65. Thibaudet, 279.
66. Cf. Conche, 83.
67. Erich Auerbach, *Mimesis: Dargestellte Wirklichkeit in der abendländischen Literatur* (Bern: A. Francke, 1946), 291.
68. Cf. Thibaudet, 350.
69. Parslow, 138-9.
70. Nolan, 135.
71. Frame, 300.
72. Ibid., 148.
73. Thibaudet, 104.
74. Cf. Frame, 119.
75. Cf. ibid., 119-21.
76. Ibid., 276.
77. Ibid. 147.
78. Ibid.
79. Ibid.
80. Ibid., 296.
81. Ibid.
82. Hallie, 126.
83. Ehrlich, 80.
84. Frame, 182.
85. Jean Starobinski, "Montaigne et la 'relation a autruy,'" *Saggi e Ricerche di Letteratura Francese* 9 (1968): 90.
86. Ibid., 92.
87. Cf. Ehrlich, 43.
88. Parslow, 17.
89. Traeger, 150-1.
90. Hallie, 160-1.
91. Lino Pertile, "Su alcune nuove fonti degli *Essais* di Montaigne," *Bibliothèque d'Humanisme et Renaissance* 31, 3 (septembre 1969): 492.
92. Hallie, 109.
93. Ibid.
94. Ibid.
95. Cf. Frame, 291.
96. Traeger, 155.
97. Cf. Thibaudet, 489.
98. Cf. ibid., 495.
99. Regosin, 174.

100. Ibid.
101. Ibid., 174-5.
102. Lablénie, 101-2.
103. Michaël Baraz, *L'Être et la connaissance selon Montaigne* (Toulouse: J. Corti, 1968), 171.
104. Thibaudet, 504.
105. Cf. Nolan, 96.
106. Cf. Thibaudet, 489.
107. Cf. ibid.
108. Ibid., 466.
109. Cf. Tauro, 180, 208.
110. Regosin, 174.
111. Cf. Thibaudet, 500.
112. Ibid., 71.
113. Starobinski, "Montaigne et la 'relation...,'" 94-5.
114. Thibaudet, 383.
115. Regosin, 173.
116. Ibid.
117. Ibid., 174.
118. Michel Butor, *Essais sur les "Essais"* (Paris: Gallimard, 1968), 61.
119. Lablénie, 103.
120. Ibid.
121. Cf. Conche, 58.

BIBLIOGRAPHY

Auerbach, Erich. *Mimesis: Dargestellte Wirklichkeit in der abendländischen Literatur*. Bern: A. Francke, 1946.

Baraz, Michaël. *L'Être et la connaissance selon Montaigne*. Paris: J. Corti, 1968.

_____. "Les Images dans les *Essais* de Montaigne." *Bibliothèque d'Humanisme et Renaissance* 27, 2 (mai 1969): 361-94.

Battista, Anna Maria. *Alle origine del pensiero politico libertino: Montaigne e Charron* . Pubblicazioni dell'Istituto di studi storico-politici, 11. Milan: A. Giuffrè, 1966.

Beaudry, James G. "The Concept of Virtue in the *Essais* of Montaigne." Ph.D. diss., University of Illinois, 1973.

Boon, Jean-Pierre. *Montaigne, gentilhomme et essayiste*. Encyclopédie universitaire. Paris: Éditions Universitaires, 1971.

Bowen, Barbara C. *The Age of Bluff: Paradox and Ambiguity in Rabelais and Montaigne*. Illinois Studies in Language and Literature, 62. Urbana: Univ. of Illinois Press, 1972.

Bowman, Frank P. *Montaigne: Essays*. London: E. Arnold, 1965.

Butor, Michel. *Essais sur les "Essais."* Les Essais, 133. Paris: Gallimard, 1968.

Cameron, Keith. "Montaigne and the Mask." *L'Esprit Créateur* 8 (fall 1968): 198-207.

Conche, Marcel. *Montaigne ou la conscience heureuse*. Philosophes de tous les temps, 14. Paris: Séghers, 1966.

Dubois, Claude-Gilbert. *Mythe et langage au seizième siècle*. Collections Ducros, 8. Bordeaux: Ducros, 1970.

Ehrlich, Hélène-Hédy. *Montaigne: la critique et le langage*. Paris: Klincksieck, 1972.

Frame, Donald M. *Montaigne: A Biography*. New York: Harcourt, Brace and World, 1965.

_____. *Montaigne's Discovery of Man: The Humanization of a Humanist*. New York: Columbia Univ. Press, 1955.

Friedrich, Hugo. *Montaigne*, trans. Robert Rovini. Bibliothèque des idées. Paris: Gallimard, 1968.

Genz, Henry E. "Montaigne's Concept of 'Non-Identity' as a Basis for the Self-Portrait." *L'Esprit Créateur* 8 (fall 1968): 194-7.

Glauser, Alfred. *Montaigne paradoxal*. Paris: A.G. Nizet, 1972.

Gray, Floyd. *Le Style de Montaigne*. Paris: A.G. Nizet, 1958.

Hall, Kathleen M. "Certain Mutations: Thoughts on the Evolution of One of Montaigne's Earliest *Essais.*" *L'Esprit Créateur* 8 (fall 1968): 208-15.

Hallie, Philip P. *The Scar of Montaigne: An Essay in Personal Philosophy.* Middletown, Conn.: Wesleyan Univ. Press, 1966

Hatzfeld, Helmut A. "Per una definizione dello stile di Montaigne." *Convivium*, n.s., 3 (maggio-giugno 1954): 284-90.

Holyoake, S. John. "Further Reflections on Montaigne and the Concept of the Imagination." *Bibliothèque d'Humanisme et Renaissance* 31, 3 (septembre 1969): 495-523.

Judrin, Roger. *Montaigne et son oeuvre*. Ècrivains de tous les temps, 37. Paris: Séghers, 1971.

Lablénie, Edmond. *Essais sur Montaigne*. Paris: Société d'édition d'enseignement supérieur, 1967.

Lewis, Philip E. "L'Apologie d'une connaissance véçue." *L'Esprit Créateur* 8 (fall 1968): 219-29.

Merleau-Ponty, Maurice. "Lecture de Montaigne." *Les Temps Modernes* 27 (décembre 1947): 1044-60.

Micha, Alexandre. *Le Singulier Montaigne*. Paris: A.G. Nizet, 1964.

Montaigne, Michel de. *The Complete Essays of Montaigne,* trans. Donald M. Frame. Stanford, Calif.: Stanford Univ. Press, 1958.

_____. *Les Essais*, ed. Pierre Villey. Paris: Presses Universitaires de France, 1965.

Moreau, Pierre. *Montaigne*, 5th ed. Connaissance des lettres, 4. Paris: Hatier, 1958.

Naudeau, Olivier. *La Pensée de Montaigne et la composition des "Essais."* Travaux d'Humanisme et Renaissance, 125. Geneva: Droz, 1972.

Nolan, Donald J. "Montaigne's Use of the Comic in the *Essais*." Ph.D. diss., University of Illinois, 1967.

Parslow, Morris. "Montaigne's Composition: A Study of the Structure of the *Essays* of the Third Book." Ph.D. diss., Princeton University, 1954.

Pertile, Lino. "Su alcune nuove fonti degli *Essais* di Montaigne." *Bibliothèque d'Humanisme et Renaissance* 31, 3 (septembre 1969): 481-94.

Pouilloux, Jean-Yves. *Lire les "Essais" de Montaigne.* Les Textes à l'appui. Paris: Maspero, 1969.

Regosin, Richard. "Language and the Dialectic of the Self in Montaigne's *Essais.*" *Kentucky Romance Quarterly* 19 (1972): 67-75.

Sayce, Richard A. *The Essays of Montaigne: A Critical Exploration*. London: Weidenfeld & Nicolson, 1972.

Stapfer, Paul. *Montaigne,* 2nd ed. Les Grands Ècrivains français. Paris: Hachette, 1913.

Starobinski, Jean. "Distance et plénitude." *Mercure de France* 348 (juillet 1963): 400-9.

_____. "Montaigne en mouvement." *Nouvelle Revue Française* 8 (janvier-mars 1960): 16-22, 254-66.

_____. "Montaigne et la 'relation a autruy.'" *Saggi e Ricerche di Letteratura Francese* 9 (1968): 79-106.

Stone, Donald, Jr. "Death in the Third Book." *L'Esprit Créateur* 8 (fall 1968), 185-93.

Strowski, Fortunat. *Montaigne*, 2nd ed. New York: Lenox Hill, 1931. Reprint, New York: B. Franklin, 1971.

Tauro, Giacomo. *Montaigne*. Milan: Società editrice Dante Alighieri di Albrighi, Segati & C., 1928.

Thibaudet, Albert. *Montaigne*. Paris: Gallimard, 1963.

Traeger, Wolf Eberhard. *Aufbau und Gedankenführung in Montaignes Essays*. Heidelberg: C. Winter, 1961.

Villey, Pierre. *Les sources et l'évolution des Essais de Montaigne*, 2nd ed. 2 vols. Paris: Hachette, 1933.

_____. *Lexique de la langue des Essais de Montaigne et index des noms propres*. New York: Lenox Hill, 1933. Reprint, New York: B. Franklin, 1973.

Winegrad, Dilys Veronica. "Expression and Being and the *Essais* of Montaigne." Ph.D. diss., University of Pennsylvania, 1970.

_____. "Language as Theme and Image in the *Essais* of Montaigne." *Symposium* (Syracuse University), n.s., 28 (fall 1974): 274-83.